Using Design Protection in the
Fashion and Textile Industry

Using Design Protection in the Fashion and Textile Industry

by

ULLA VAD LANE-ROWLEY, BA (HONS)

Diploma Member of the Chartered Society of Designers

JOHN WILEY & SONS

Chichester • New York • Weinheim • Brisbane • Singapore • Toronto

Published in 1997 by John Wiley & Sons Ltd,
Baffins Lane, Chichester,
West Sussex PO19 1UD, England

National   01243 779777
International   (+44) 1243 779777
e-mail (for orders and customer service enquiries): cs-books@wiley.co.uk
Visit our Home Page on http://www.wiley.co.uk
or http://www.wiley.com

This publication is intended as an accurate and up to date overview of design protection in the fashion and
textile industry. However, it does not aim to cover all legal eventualities and is sold on the understanding
that neither the publisher nor the author is engaged in providing legal services. If legal advice or other
expert assistance is required, the services of a competent professional should be sought.

Other Wiley Editorial Offices

John Wiley & Sons, Inc., 605 Third Avenue
New York, NY 10158-0012, USA

WILEY-VCH Verlag GmbH, Pappelallee 3,
D-69469 Weinheim, Germany

Jacaranda Wiley Ltd, 33 Park Road, Milton,
Queensland 4064, Australia

John Wiley & Sons (Asia) Pte Ltd, 2 Clementi Loop #02-01,
Jin Xing Distripark, Singapore 129809

John Wiley & Sons (Canada) Ltd, 22 Worcester Road,
Rexdale, Ontario M9W IL1, Canada

Library of Congress Cataloging-in-Publication Data
Lane-Rowley, Ulla Vad.
    Using design protection in the fashion and textile industry/by Ulla Vad Lane-Rowley.
        p.   cm.
    Includes bibliographical references and index.
    ISBN 0–471–96925–7 (pbk.)
        1. Design protection–Great Britain. 2. Textile industry–Law and legislation–Great Britain. 3. Clothing
    trade–Law and legislation–Great Britain.   I. Title.
KD1345.L36   1997
346.7304'84–dc21   97–21574
                                                                                                          CIP

British Library Cataloguing in Publication Data

A catalogue record for this book is available from the British Library

ISBN 0–471–96925–7
Typeset in 12/14 pt in Bembo by Poole Typesetting (Wessex) Ltd, Bournemouth, Dorset
Printed and bound in Great Britain by Redwood Books, Trowbridge, Wiltshire
This book is printed on acid-free paper responsibly manufactured from sustainable forestation, for which at
least two trees are planted for each one used for paper production.

To my husband Colin – min Skat,

My greatest thanks and appreciation for your never ending support and encouragement as well as the constructive feedback and brilliant 'round the table' brainstorming.

– også Tak til min Danske Familie!

CONTENTS

GLOSSARY

©	Copyright
®	Registered trade mark
™	Trade mark (typically used for unregistered trade marks)
CTM	Community trade mark (EU legislation)
CDPA	Copyright, Designs and Patents Act 1988 (UK legislation)
DACS	Design and Artists Copyright Society
GATT	General Agreement on Tariffs and Trade
EPO	European Patent Office
EPC	European Patent Convention
EU	European Union
FDPA	Fashion Design Protection Association
IP	Intellectual Property
OHIM	Office for Harmonisation in the Internal Market (EU trade mark registry)
PCT	Patent Co-operation Treaty (basis for granting worldwide patents)
R&D	Research and development
TMA	Trade Marks Act 1994 (UK legislation)
TRIPs	Trade-Related Aspects of Intellectual Property Rights (international agreement 1995)
WIPO	World Intellectual Property Organisation—specialist agency established 1974 by the United Nations to co-ordinate the international conventions for intellectual property
WTO	World Trade Organisation

ACKNOWLEDGEMENTS

Special acknowledgement and thanks are given to the following for their qualified advice and invaluable contributions—without these the book would not have been possible: Denzil Cowdry, Lewis R. Goodman, Gina Holt BA (Hons) PGCE as well as the following:

Anti Copying in Design (ACID), Simon Clark.
British Copyright Council, London.
Chartered Society of Designers (CSD), Mr Geoffrey Adams, London.
Commission of the European Communities, London.
Design and Artists Copyright Society, Umesh Mistry, Collective Rights Dept.
Drapers Record, Sophie Hewitt-Jones, Editor.
Fashion Design Protection Associates Ltd, Achilleas Constantinou, Chairman.
Patent Office, The, including all sections of the Copyright Directorate, Design Registry and Trade Mark Registry, London and Newport/Gwent.
Payment and Clearances (Administration) Ltd, Association of (APACS), London.
Solo Syndication Ltd, London.
World Trade Organisation, Intellectual Property and Investment Division, Geneva/Switzerland.

Special acknowledgement is given to the following fashion companies and textile organisations:

Courtaulds Fibres/Tencel Fibres Europe, Simon Baker, Marketing.

Dupont De Nemours International SA, Switzerland.

Dupont (UK), Kit Blake, UK Marketing Manager.

H Flude & Co. (Hinckley) Ltd, Leicester, UK.

Harris Tweed Authority, The, Mary Macdonald.

Henry Bertrand, Edward Gilbert, Managing Director.

International Wool Secretariat, M I Piercy, Group Manager Woolmark Services.

J&J Crombie, David Noakes, Marketing.

Levi Strauss (UK) Ltd (Press Office), Shilland & Co., London.

Monsoon Ltd, Peter Simons, Chairman, Head Office, London.

Premiére Vision/PB Marketing (UK), Patricia Lambert.

Puffa Ltd, Victor Rosenberg, Managing Director.

Slix Ltd, Victoria Enright, Sales Support Manager.

Stowaway, Rosemary Moore, Designer and Managing Director.

'Strawberry Fields' Clothes for Kids, Danielle Metzstein, Proprietor.

Timberland (UK) Ltd, Debbie Urquhart, Marketing Operations Manager.

FOREWORD

Today's successful textile and apparel manufacturers know that the last two decades have been marked by an accelerating rate of industrial change in at least two aspects—firstly, the development of the global market, with often sudden and sustained competition from unexpected parts of the world and secondly, the recognition that investment in the latest technology whether it be in spinning or sewing equipment or in quality assurance and management systems is available to all. This is of course largely taken for granted by customers. These productivity attributes now rarely command 'favoured nation' treatment from buyers. They have their repercussion of the design scene.

What then differentiates one producer from another? Price and design.

As to the former, it is wise to bear in mind Ruskin's dictum that 'There is hardly anything in the world that some men cannot make a little worse and sell a little cheaper and the people who consider price only are this man's lawful prey'. Quality and value for money are the first important plus for successful producers. Design is the remaining plus that provides the competitive edge. Given these two requirements it is inevitably the case that many international traders and manufacturers will aim to go after the more profitable fashion business. Fashion has been described as the segment of the market with more than four seasons and thus more than four inventory changes a year! It relies on continual design changes.

Good design is therefore a precious asset to be protected. To be fashion right is very much a matter of understanding and interpreting trends. Alas when speed is of the essence, the designer in his entrepreneurial role may well unwittingly transgress the bounds of copy or intellectual property rights.

This book will create an awareness which should help manufacturers to avoid such pitfalls while underlining one's own rights. Even in the less fashionable sectors of the textile and apparel business there is the need to rise to the 'Quick Response' and 'Just in Time' demands from retailers and others. The effect is to compress the various stages in the design process into an ever shorter time span, and at all times it is essential to protect the investment in the creative process in order to maintain the lead over one's competitors, and also to protect that lead.

In view of the pressures of this competitive age this book is a timely contribution helping to better understand, defend and use the varied mass of 'do's and don'ts' in the field of textile and apparel intellectual property. Its non-legal language should give it a place on every manager's and designer's bookshelf.

Lewis R. Goodman OBE, Comp T.I.

PREFACE

The prime objective and purpose of this book is to provide the fashion industry and individuals who work with commercial design with an up-to-date framework and general understanding of the current rights and legislation available to the clothing industry for the protection of innovative textile and garment designs.

The focus will initially be on UK legislation as introduced through the Copyright, Designs and Patents Act 1988 (CDPA) and the Trade Marks Act 1994 (TMA) to provide the reader with a foundation and understanding of the home market in the UK. Then the book continues to expand and outline the intellectual property developments both in the European and international market-places which are, to an increasing extent, being used by British companies, either for sourcing materials and production facilities or as export markets.

The quite complex subject of design protection and intellectual property is covered in a book structure which provides the reader with an understanding of the basic principles and rules of the current protection for industrial design. The book has been written in very accessible language to allow it to be used as an initial reference point in the day-to-day work of business managers, designers and others concerned with intellectual property rights, illustrating and explaining the mechanics, time and cost involved in making use of the range of different protection types in existence. Throughout the book there are examples and case studies that specifically deal with the textile and fashion industry, to help the reader understand how the law is applied in today's business environment in real terms.

Intellectual property rights are covered mainly from the aspect of the application made of industrial design in the clothing industry—as applied to commercial quantity production on a commercial scale—as opposed to focus on unique pieces created by artists or craftsmen for very limited production runs. The latter type of artistic design is however included where applicable, i.e. under the section concerned with automatic copyright.

Part of the book is also concerned with the various issues of why companies need to be concerned with design protection in the first place and how to deal with infringement and unauthorised copying. Ways of maximising the protection of a company's intellectual property include copyright, design right, registered design, trade mark protection and in a few exceptional cases patent registration, which this book will describe in the following chapters.

The growing number of UK copyright cases reported by the fashion trade press and financial papers indicate that many companies do not realise the full implications of current legislation and standards applied in this field, thereby losing out financially, by not protecting their products sufficiently or, on the other hand, having to realise the full impact of design infringement or direct copying when being sued by the design originator.

In the commercial experience of the writer—having been involved in the clothing industry since 1987—it has been found that designers and management can be quite hazy about the distinct applications and differences between patents, design rights, copyright, trade marks and other legislation available to protect the design of a garment. In many cases the subject of 'intellectual property' is found by the designer or manager to be too complex, time consuming and written in quite inaccessible language which in a busy day-to-day environment takes too long to grasp fully in order to make effective use of the legislative framework available for the fashion industry.

Instead businesses often continue with an attitude of 'let's hope for the best' albeit with a general lack of knowledge and considerable confusion regarding the fundamental action and costs required to register designs whilst also being unclear of the UK statutory protection available—which is achieved *automatically* upon creation of a design—and for which design protection can be considerably strengthened by simple business practices in the design room environment.

The viewpoint that businesses must increase their knowledge of intellectual property rights was expressed earlier in 1991 by the Fashion

Design Protection Association (published in the trade journal *Drapers Record*): 'We are astonished at how many designers still do not know that they can protect their designs. They really need to wise up and get some expert advice'.

The problem of design protection was already recognised by the UK Government in a 1983 Green Paper concerned with intellectual property in the statement 'compared to our main competitors, there is insufficient awareness of the importance and value of intellectual property rights. The rights are relatively inaccessible because their use is complex, costly and time consuming. The procedures give the impression of an arcane world rather than of a modern technological Britain'.

As a result more accessible legislation was introduced with the CDPA in 1988. Further improvements were introduced via the Trade Marks Act 1994, primarily to implement an EC harmonisation directive as well as closing certain loopholes in UK trade marks law and generally extending the trade mark protection available to trading brand names.

Since 1983 considerable attention has been directed towards the field of intellectual property and design, an example being the Design Council's exhibition in 1985 'Fair or Foul', which illustrated the extent to which British industry had to face up to copying and counterfeiting, not only in Britain but in world markets. Later, in 1989 the 'Design Museum' opened in London's Docklands, dedicated to mass-produced goods with an emphasis on design. Supported by the designer entrepreneur Sir Terence Conran, the Museum's purpose is to promote 'awareness of the importance of design in education, industry, commerce and culture'.

While the British clothing and fashion textile industry may be starting to come to terms with and act upon the copying of products in the home market-place at European level EU countries started discussion in 1991 of a 'Green Paper on the Legal Protection of Industrial Design' and moves in 1996 involved the debate of the matured proposal for new Community legislation. But until the proposal comes into force, an industrial design product may still only achieve European intellectual protection through the variety of different national legislations, thereby maintaining the complexity of effective design protection. Once EU legislation becomes a reality it should greatly help to improve the ease with which the fashion industry may make use of European intellectual property legislation when exporting within the European Community. In the meantime companies may want to make use of the new EU trade mark registration system, which allows a brand name to be protected throughout the EU by one single registration with OHIM, the European trade mark registry office in Alicante, Spain.

During the last GATT negotiations which were completed in 1994, known as the Uruguay Round, the GATT member countries concluded an agreement entitled Trade-Related Aspects of Intellectual Property Rights, also known as the TRIPs agreement. An outline summary of this new treaty is found in Chapter 7. TRIPs came into force in January 1995 and has undergone review discussions during the Ministerial Conference in Singapore in December 1996 to assess how well the initial treaty addressed the subject at an international level.

The subject and framework of intellectual property (IP) rights, by the use of arcane legal language, often remain somewhat inaccessible and not exactly user-friendly for groups of individuals directly involved in working with fashion design. In the process of trying to understand such a legal field, it is hoped that this book will go some considerable way to assist the general understanding of the subject and make it easier for small to medium size fashion companies as well as individual designers to apply design protection in their day-to-day business.

However, due to the fact that intellectual property rights, including design protection, is an area which undergoes continuous revision, changes and implementation via new legislation—both at UK, European and international levels—it is important that this book is *not* seen as a definitive or exhaustive account of the law concerning intellectual property and protection issues. Rather, it is intended as a work for initial reference—an accessible directory—which will provide a framework and understanding of the basic principles and rules of current protection for industrial design.

The foundation for this book is based on information available to the public through government bodies such as The Patent Office, the Commission of the European Communities and the World Trade Organisation (WTO). Further sources of information include trade and professional organisations concerned with design protection and trade publications, published after the introduction of major new UK legislation notably the Copyright, Designs and Patents Act 1988.

It is the aim of the book to help save considerable time for anybody working with product development and design protection in the fashion and textile industry, by pulling together and presenting the wide spectrum of intellectual property rights available via current legislation and to illustrate 'how it works' by including a number of 'real life' case studies from the fashion industry and to make the reader aware of new developments and organisations where further information may be obtained on the subject.

For many designers and fashion companies it will be true that in general it may only be necessary to make use of one or two of the IP categories, e.g. statutory design rights and/or registered trade mark registration. However, it was a conscious decision to include all main IP categories in the book to allow individual readers to seek as much and the broadest possible information before making the decision to use one particular type or form of design protection. Also, individuals working with original, industrial design and/or branded product ranges may find that in some instances one category, e.g. statutory design rights will offer sufficient protection, while in other cases more long-term and official registration may be required such as design registration, depending on various design and business factors such as level of design originality, anticipated product life cycle and sales volume of an industrial design.

In other instances, a business may find that registered trade mark protection offers a better degree of general business protection which may be equal or even more valuable than individual design protection, e.g. in very fast changing fashion companies where designs change four to eight times a year but the brand name remains as *the* consistent product element throughout several years. Therefore, where companies make substantial investments in highly branded ranges it can be more beneficial to protect the ongoing brand name and related artwork which differentiate products in the market-place.

The book covers quite diverse IP categories such as copyright, design right, patents, registered design and registered trade marks, however this does *not* mean that all categories are of equal importance to all areas of original design and development of industrial design products. The particular application of an IP category is instead highlighted within each field with examples and general guidelines.

On the subject of intellectual property rights in the UK, a number of previous publications originate from the legal profession, approaching the subject from predominantly legal backgrounds and covering *all* industries working with industrial design. In contrast this book is written specifically for the design sector of fashion/textile industries. The writer's context in dealing with the various topics in this book is to take the starting point from product development, design and the commercial environment of today's fashion industry. In approaching design and copyright protection from this perspective the special requirements of clothing industries are addressed throughout the text and illustrated via case studies and business contributions.

SUMMARY

The development of copyright legislation: Chapter 1

The first chapter gives a brief outline of the legislative evolution of intellectual property protection from its very early days in the 15th century. Linked to the introduction of the literary printing process in Europe, the first effective step towards exclusive legal rights involved a 'letter of patent' issued by the sovereign and used to a certain extent to exercise control of publications. Since then, industrial developments rapidly gained pace towards an industrial revolution and a more complex legislative framework became necessary to meet the very diverse requirements by various industries to protect different types of intellectual property via copyright, design right, patents, registered design and trade mark protection.

In this century, in step with the growing scale of international business transactions and export levels, a number of international copyright conventions have developed including new European legislation for trade marks and industrial design protection, as well as the wider reaching TRIPs agreement of 1995 under the World Trade Organisation, involving over 123 countries worldwide.

Why be concerned with design protection?: Chapter 2

Whereas plagiarism of design products does not require any sophisticated know-how, developing original design products requires a considerable amount of time and costs which arise from research and development of the new products.

The function and purpose of intellectual property legislation is *not* merely to present business management and designers with another tiresome obstacle in the day-to-day running of a company, but to offer industry an effective tool to safeguard investments made in new products. In return, design proprietor(s)—as well as trade mark owners—can, to a great extent, ensure that earnings from the commercial exploitation of original work does not benefit pirates and imitators.

The use and application of legislation has become more accessible for companies, together with the UK Government's updating of the law through the Copyright, Designs and Patents Act 1988 and the Trade Marks Act 1994 making the legal field more 'user-friendly'. As a result a growing number of UK industries are making active use of design protection law and a higher number of cases concerning the clothing industry have been highlighted in the trade press.

Intellectual property and ownership: Chapter 3

When an organisation is claiming intellectual property of its original work, certain business practices should be adopted to reduce the risk of exposing the design to potential copying opportunities.

The company or individuals must be aware of the possible consequences of:

1. **Premature disclosure** which can disqualify original work being granted a registration, be it for a design registration or a technical patent registration.
2. **Exact ownership** of design in the instance of employing designers, when commissioning freelance designers or when buying designs from outside companies, i.e. textile designs for garment production.

Furthermore, managers and designers must ensure they are keeping up to date with recent developments and innovations within the industry, to avoid spending resources on 'redeveloping' already existing concepts. This includes searching databases of both registered and alternative unregistered concepts to make sure an identical or highly similar concept does not already exist. Searches can be carried out by the Patent Office, the Design Registry and the Trade Mark Register. Independent and some newly formed search agencies will have access to databases which hold information of little known or unregistered brand names. A company that has traded and become known, over time, to customers and local industry under its own unregistered trade mark will be able to claim certain rights in its trade mark, compared to a brand name which may have been devised at a later date by a company or individual unaware of the unregistered trade mark's existence.

Once the company publishes/markets the design, in the case of registered designs, registered trade marks and patents—as well as for automatic copyright/© material—it will be useful to mark the product with a registration number (e.g. for registered design, patents or trade marks if applicable) and the type of ownership such as © for copyright claim in products or ™ and ® for trade marks, thereby strengthening the company's position in a legal dispute. By marking articles, a proprietor is clearly communicating particular ownership rights and the infringer is prevented from claiming a defence of 'innocence' or being unaware of any ownership claims linked to a particular product. Although such marking is not required by law in the UK, some countries do require appropriate marking—of the ownership type, name or owner and the year of publication.

Intellectual property legislation and IP categories in the UK: Chapter 4

Statutory rights in the UK arise by legislative provision automatically when a work is created, with no need for official recording. The two categories of unregistered protection rights available to designers and companies in the UK under the latest 1988 legislation are copyright and design right.

Copyright: comes into operation automatically when an original drawing or work is created (including computer generated works). It applies to artistic works which include original works by artistic craftsmanship.

The advantage of copyright arising automatically is that it does not involve any time or cost consuming formal registration procedures.

The purpose of copyright claim is to prevent the reproduction of a work—be it completely, in part or adapted form—without the permission of the creator/owner's consent. Alternatively, the copyright holder may seek financial remedy for any such reproductions.

Copyright will last for the lifetime of the creator plus 70 years thereafter. In the case of infringement it is the responsibility of the creator to prove the ownership and existence of copyright and that the work has been copied. For that purpose, when working with original design it is strongly recommended that companies install simple in-house design records to prove ownership and date of creation.

More than one copyright can exist, for a highly similar work, if each creator has arrived at the work independently. Copyright does *not* cover works where the underlying design is non-artistic, however three-dimensional *artistic* works where copyright does apply include sculptures, *models* and *works of artistic craftsmanship*.

Where copyright protected work is reproduced in larger quantities or by industrial processes, articles are regarded as 'industrial design'. And although copyright may protect the *drawing* of an industrial design of artistic merit, it does not generally protect the industrial article. In cases of industrially produced designs one should instead make use of 'design rights' which deal specifically with the industrial application of design products.

Fields in the fashion industry where copyright ownership is applicable include two-dimensional design work such as original sketches (except sketches of the shape of a garment of little or no aesthetic quality), fashion illustrations, textile design, surface design, dressmaking patterns, labels, transfers and trade advertisements, plus garments of such pure artistic merit that they qualify as artistic works, e.g. garments produced only once or twice as unique items of craftsmanship.

Design right: is a new protection type introduced by the 1988 Act to offer protection for original, industrial design articles. Protection is given to the shape or configuration (whether internal or external) of the whole *or part* of the designed article.

Design right protection is concerned with *original* industrial design, focusing on the actual article and without any mandatory requirement for original drawings to claim ownership, *unless* that was how the design was first recorded. Alternatively, three-dimensional articles such as prototype or production garments of the design can be used to prove design right, together with material proving first marketing/publication date, promotional adverts and PR catalogues.

Design right protection lasts for up to 10 years from the first date of marketing—or 15 years if not made available commercially—with the exclusive rights to reproduce the design, subject to any 'licence of right' provisions during the last five years of the 10-year protection period from first marketing date. 'Licence of right' can be obtained by other companies who are obliged to pay royalties for the licence.

Design right for industrial design is *copyright-based* allowing the owner the exclusive right to produce articles to a particular design, but it is not a monopoly-based right for original industrial design (as opposed to registered designs).

The UK design right is a particularly British protection type not found in other countries, and as such is not supported by any international copyright conventions. In individual European countries the gap in the protection of industrial design is in some instances covered by various short-term protection categories, e.g. 'petty patents' or 'utility models' with some formal registration systems rather than automatic protection rights. However, recent legislative developments within the European Union (see Chapter 7) will in the near future facilitate protection of original industrial designs via Community design protection, valid throughout all EU Member States.

Registered protection rights: Chapter 5

There are certain formalities and requirements involved in obtaining registered protection which are covered in this chapter. Apart from the direct cost of preparing documents and design representations, it must be remembered that in most instances legal assistance will be required, to ensure the predominantly written registration will be legally 'watertight' with no loopholes for potential copy infringement.

The product elements which are protected by each registration category have been clearly defined by current UK legislation ranging from strictly functional concepts for patents to aesthetic aspects of a product design protected via registered design.

In relation to registered design, the intellectual proprietor(s) should not only view the registration costs or direct expenses, but also be clear about the actual requirements of the business and the purpose of registering the design, be it to exercise monopoly of a new design concept, enable licensing and/or to protect the existing as well as long-term trading environment, or future business fields via product/brand diversification.

The latest Trade Marks Act, introduced in 1994, offers a much wider protection and improved enforcement rights for brand name and logos which, in the environment of competitive fashion industries, is vital. On the basis that while the product ranges of fashion change from season to season, brand name and trade marks are viewed as the continuing asset upon which business is built in the long term, also considering that the majority of the industry is trading in markets where strong brand loyalty exists.

The definition of a trade mark, under the TMA 1994, now spans more widely than merely covering the brand name and logo. It can also cover product elements such as 'shape', 'colour' and perhaps less applicable for fashion products 'sound' and 'smell', subject to certain limitations/exceptions detailed further within Chapter 5.

How to deal with design infringement: Chapter 6

Several types of action can be taken by the design and/or trade mark owner to stop the illegal activities of counterfeiting and passing off. Predominantly, prevention will be better than cure, e.g. by drawing up contracts with all suppliers and various sub-contractors—both within the UK and overseas—that clearly state the terms and IP obligations under which business is to be carried out between the intellectual property owner and any supplier/manufacturer. In the case of competitors selling infringing designs, a considerable range of copyright organisations, lawyers specialising in IP legislation and trading standards departments will be able to advise on the action to be taken and to assess whether to pursue legal action.

A decisive factor in pursuing legal action in infringement cases is still the potential level of costs involved. Litigation can leave individual designers and smaller companies producing original designs engulfed by legal fees when instigated by financially stronger but less innovative competitors. For this reason membership of copyright protection organisations and legal insurance to cover litigation fees can prove crucial. Other long-term benefits in taking up membership with a copyright protection association include being able to keep up to date with legislative developments, having access to the organisation's confidential consultancy services and/or specialist legal advisers, provision of expert witnesses for legal evidence and the use of the copyright organisation's logo on business and promotional material as a deterrent against possible counterfeiters.

In the event of discovering potential infringements of designs or trade marks certain preliminary and practical measures should be taken to assess if, in accordance with current legislation, there is a case of infringement to be defended. The preliminary measures which should be taken include, if possible, the purchase of at least one of the offending garments/articles. Then, the matter should be placed immediately before legal advisers for a balanced assessment of the legal strengths, weaknesses and risk factors of the alleged infringement.

If it is decided to proceed with further action to stop the production and sale of copies, first with the support of legal advisers the company should ensure to explore and make every effort to settle the dispute. Should all efforts fail at this stage further remedies against counterfeiting include:

1. INTERLOCUTORY INJUNCTION—to halt the production and sale of imitation products.
2. OBTAINING EVIDENCE VIA A COURT ORDER—used in cases to force the co-operation of an alleged infringer.
3. 'ANTON PILLER' COURT ORDER—used in exceptional instances to allow the plaintiff or the legal advisers to search and access the defendant's premises including stock, documents and other valuable evidence.
4. COUNTERFEITING SEIZURE—the right of seizure can be used in particular instances where a street trader or similar outlet of copies does not have a permanent or regular place of business. Advance notification must be made to the local police authorities.
5. COURT ACTION UNDER CIVIL OR CRIMINAL LAW—depending on the type of evidence, level of illegal and/or criminal offence by the infringing party and according to how 'watertight' allegations are, legal action can be taken under civil or criminal law. In general, civil action tends to take longer and be more costly, compared to criminal action where cases may be settled within weeks and carry heavy fines and possible jail sentences for convicted defendants.
6. FINAL INJUNCTION—following a successful court action a final restraining order will usually be issued by the court to prevent the defending party from producing any further copies or committing any other acts of infringement. Also, decisions will be made regarding the infringing goods/materials, e.g. to be destroyed or handed over to the plaintiff.
7. MONETARY CLAIMS—the court will decide, based on calculations, the level of damages to be awarded to the plaintiff following a successful action. The underlying principle is that the intellectual property owner should be no worse off had the infringement not taken place.

While all of the above remedies are available to take action against various infringements, prevention rather than cure is strongly recommended. As illustrated by the business strategies and campaigns developing from many well-known fashion companies, by clearly showing that a company—or individual designer—takes its intellectual property rights seriously and will not tolerate copying, a deterrent factor is created for possible infringers to think twice. At the same time, educating and informing consumers of the financial effects of supporting ill-produced copies will, in the longer term, hopefully eliminate any demand for cheap counterfeit articles.

Design protection in the European single market: Chapter 7

With the increased economic integration of European countries it would seem only logical that the single market should operate one Community design protection legislation rather than numerous sets of national laws.

The obvious advantages of common EU legislation are visible through the Community Trade Mark legislation enforced in January 1996. The CTM 1996 is applied as the common foundation for each EC Member State to bring its own trade mark law up to date within the same legal structure and trade mark criteria, thereby making it substantially easier for trade mark owners in future to protect their brand names and take legal action if necessary throughout the EU when exporting to other member countries.

For the purpose of protecting original design concepts, substantial legislative developments are taking place on a European scale. The proposed EU Regulation in 1994 (94C 29/02) together with a Directive of 1996 (subject to amendments and final approval), are likely in the near future to introduce protection types for a Community design system.

The new design protection will introduce unregistered design rights similar to UK design rights, though the EC version limits protection to three years. All designs which are to benefit from Community design rights must satisfy certain requirements of representing new and distinctive designs.

A period of grace for the first 12 months of a design publication/ product marketing, will allow companies to market test designs prior to Community design registration. This concept gives companies and/or design owners the opportunity to assess a design's commercial value and decide either to strengthen the design protection through registration or whether the unregistered design valid for three years will be sufficient for the product's life cycle.

Should a design prove to be particularly successful within the period of grace, the more long-term design protection from a Community design registration may be required. Whereas unregistered original designs only obtain the right of preventing others from copying or otherwise infringing the design, a registration will grant the holder exclusive design ownership rights. The initial registration will be valid for five years and renewable up to a maximum of 25 years.

International markets: The WTO Agreement for intellectual property: TRIPs: Chapter 8

The Agreement on Trade-Related Aspects of Intellectual Property Rights (TRIPs)—part of the GATT Uruguay Agreement—has brought the issues of intellectual property to the forefront of intergovernmental co-operation. The TRIPs agreement came into force in January 1996, however the high level of diversity between different country members' legislations means that full implementation of the international IP agreement will require considerable time. Hence, the provision of a transitional period between one, four and 10 years for different levels of countries to adjust and establish a general legal framework which will satisfy the TRIPs structure, although significant changes are already taking place. Only two months after the Uruguay GATT agreement (including TRIPs) had been signed company managers noticed 'countries like Korea, India, Malaysia and China much more helpful . . . (than in the past)' with the whole area of intellectual property in consumer goods industries starting to shift rapidly.

On a larger scale, governmental bodies are proceeding to ensure various countries meet and adhere to the obligations of the TRIPs agreement. The general implications during the transitional time will be to test the value of the WTO rules and ensure individual nations adhere to the agreement.

In practical terms, while new international IP agreements continue to develop, the outline for the UK and EU countries seems to give a clear indication that substantial protection of intellectual property *is* a realistic option for designers and businesses who want to protect their design and brand name assets effectively. This is supported by the overall trend both in the UK and in the European market for legislation to become accessible and more 'user-friendly', to ensure designers and commercial management are able to apply and make use of the legislation as a business tool for protecting design investments.

Details of the several organisations and IP information points are found in the Address List at the end of the book.

Information for overseas countries may have to be obtained directly from national patent offices or the WTO central register for national legislation, while an initial point of reference for many UK intellectual property owners will be the Patent Office. The central enquiry desk will be able to assist with most queries in any field of intellectual property, or alternatively be able to advise which organisation to contact for further legal advice.

1

THE DEVELOPMENT OF COPYRIGHT LEGISLATION

Before starting to look at the legislative evolution of intellectual property rights, from its early days to today's design protection, it is worth considering that over the two centuries between 1709 and 1911, in the field of copyright alone some **40 Acts** were introduced in the UK. The large number of new legislation sanctions were introduced to enlarge the scope required by numerous technological developments over this period of time.

In order to understand the complexity of the subject and the individual Acts which cover very diverse industries and products, the introduction of current UK law can be viewed as follows: the current UK copyright legislation Act of 1988 (CDPA) was initiated back in 1974 with the Whitford Committee which, after hearing massive representations from interested parties, produced a 274-page report. In July 1981, the Government issued a Green Paper and it took another eight years for the White Paper approval by Parliament, with the actual implementation of the new law taking place in 1989. So the total time span for introducing the 1988 Act was in reality **15 years!**

As mentioned in the Preface, the writer's aim is not to provide an exhaustive account of all past and present issues and numerous amounts of legislation concerning intellectual property rights. However, to support the understanding and application of design protection in current business environments, this chapter is concerned with the beginning of protection rights and major developments which have been the foundation for today's UK legislation.

Under current UK legislation, the two main categories which offer protection for original works are:

- **Statutory rights—copyright and design right**. These can exist from the moment when the original work is first drawn or outlined in a tangible design document. Although each category covers specific areas and types of design, both relate to the author's right to control and authorise any copying or variation of a design.
- **Registered rights—patents, registered design** and **registered trade marks**. Protection under registered rights is based on monopoly rights as opposed to control of copyright-based rights. Although these categories involve certain formalities, time and cost factors, they generally represent stronger legal rights.

Note that the UK legislation applies only within its own jurisdiction. IP protection in other EU and overseas countries is instead achieved via international or the individual country's national legislation (see Chapters 7 and 8).

1.1 Copyright development

The word 'copyright' does not merely indicate the right to copy, but is the ownership of and right to control all possible creative ways of reproducing a 'work' in particular, applied to literary, dramatic and artistic works (including paintings, drawings, photographs, sound recordings, films and various productions via new technology). Copyright law prevents reproduction, be it the entire work or a substantial part thereof, without the copyright owner's consent.

Copyright protection laws first appeared in the 15th century when the printing process was introduced to England. The copy production, predominantly of literary works, then became relatively easy. Increasing demand for copies led to development of the printing business which required the necessity of protecting the printer against piracy of his production, if his business was to flourish. In England the earliest law concerned with copyright protection was the Statute of Monopolies from 1624. One of very few pieces of legislation to predate the English system of monopoly was the Venetian Patent Ordinance created in 1474.

1.2 Letters of patent

This was the first effective step towards exclusive legal rights and a 'letter of patent' was granted by the sovereign as the sole right to reproduce *specific* works, because control over printing was particularly important to the Crown, with the need for political censorship and the potential income which it could attract.

The letter of patent was generally awarded to the printer, though in some instances granted to the actual author, who, in turn, transferred his rights to a printer or publisher, for a financial consideration naturally. With the exclusive right—which in fact was the right of total monopoly—followed the obligation to deposit a copy or copies with the Royal Library and other specified libraries.

1.3 Charter of the Stationers' Company 1556

This Charter granted by the Star Chamber Decree of 1556, allowed only members of the Stationers' Company (bookbinders, printers and booksellers) the privilege of publishing and importing copies of books, ballads, maps, pictures, sermons and so on by payment of a registration fee to the company.

However, the primary purpose of the constitution was not to protect authors, or encourage literary production but rather to control the printing and distribution of printed matter in the interests of the church and state. Through the medium of the Stationers' Company the then Government could exercise the necessary control and censorship by only allowing registration of what was considered 'suitable material'.

1.4 The Statute of Anne 1710

The next major development came via Parliament introducing the Statute of Anne 1709 implemented in April 1710. Under the title 'An Act for the Encouragement of Learning by Copies of Printed Books . . . ', copyright ownership, as known by modern law, was now assigned to the author.

To ensure that suit of infringement could be pursued, copyright owners had to register the work with the Stationers' Company (no longer favouring members of the Company) as well as depositing a copy with prescribed libraries.

Provisions in the new statute regarding literary pirates stated that pirates 'were to forfeit their copies to the proprietor of the copy, who was to make waste paper of them', furthermore the pirate was to pay to the owner one half penny, and to the Queen another half penny, for every infringing sheet found in the pirate's possession.

A new Act—the Universities Copyright Act 1775—strengthened the provisions of the Statute of Anne. However, no longer were deposits or registration a source for obtaining copyright ownership. Instead, publication of the work was sufficient to secure statutory copyright.

Legal developments outside the United Kingdom in the 18th century included the first American patent law in 1790 and the introduction by France of a patent law in 1791. Between the years 1800–82 patent laws were introduced on national levels in most European countries. Towards the end of the 19th century other notable developments included the British Trade Mark Registry—the first in the world—which opened for business in 1876. This official Registry was created following demands from businessmen for a system which would protect their products from unscrupulous traders who were passing off imitations of the genuine articles.

1.5 Developments into the 20th century

Over the years the duration of copyright protection available through legislation Acts has expanded from seven years to 70 years after the death of the author. Other provisions made by new legislations have extended copyright beyond books and printing to cover also other creative artistic and aesthetic material. These were designed to help cover various new types of works and dealing with unfair competition issues in relation to the exploitation of developing technologies.

The increasing pace of invention and industrial development in the Victorian period led to the first Patent Act in 1852—with the main focus and concern for inventions with construction or functional qualities, applicable for industry. The Act was renewed in 1949 and again in 1977, the latter Act being introduced to bring British law in line with European and international thinking, and enabling ratification to be made of international treaties.

Other individual copyright Acts which had been introduced between the years 1734–1862, individually covering specific artistic fields such as engraving, sculpture, music, drama, fine arts, etc., were repealed by a single Copyright Act in 1911. Developments taking place in the UK to support the general use of design in industry include the establishment of the Council of Industrial Design (1944) and the journal *Design* first published in 1949.

At European level the Council of Europe proposed in 1949 that an intergovernmental European Patent Office (EPO) should be established.

Following a number of conferences to unify national legislations and set up the European patent system, 16 countries signed the Community Patent Convention in 1973 which came into force in October 1977. Other developments include the quite recent legislation which now makes it possible to obtain European trade mark registration by one single application—as opposed to seeking registration in individual countries in the EU. Similar developments are taking place for introducing EU legislation concerning Community design for original industrial design products. Details of the proposed EU Directive (subject to final approval and amendments) are found in Chapter 7.

Throughout the 20th century UK developments in the field of intellectual property have drawn up clear distinctions between:

1. original and artistic work involving craftsmanship, i.e. for 'one of a kind' and *haute couture* designs protected by copyright;
2. inventions of purely functional character—for patent protection;
3. original industrial design produced for commercial use which may obtain statutory design right and/or official design registration.

Depending on the product and other circumstances which are presented in the following chapters, a product may be covered by several types of protection offering different degrees of effective protection. The main elements introduced by legislative Acts during this century include:

1. *1949 Act*. Laid the foundation for registered design and introduced the '50 rule': works produced in less than 50 units generally qualifying as artistic design. While production quantities larger than 50 are classified as 'industrial design'.
2. *1968 Act*. The Design Copyright Act gave recognition of industrial design to include artistic elements, despite being produced in quantities larger than 50. As a result, ordinary copyright now covered both artistic designs as well as industrial designs. Industrial design could achieve copyright protection for 15 years, while for artistic design copyright could be maintained for 50 years after the author's death. The different copyright time-scale was based on the aspect that industrial design, produced in larger quantities, was likely to recover development and investment costs faster than the small-scale productions of artistic design.

The broader coverage of copyright application severely increased the complexity of the law, making it extremely difficult for laymen to understand and apply the protection rights. Furthermore the legislation— in cases of copyright infringement—required the design originator to prove deliberate copying of his product by the counterfeiting party.

By the early 1970s government bodies realised that if the intellectual property legislation was to operate effectively, more accessible legislation was required for the industries and individuals whom the law was intended to serve. The review initiated by a government appointed committee in 1974 resulted in the introduction of the current law of the Copyright, Designs and Patents Act 1988.

In 1994 a new Trade Marks Act was introduced primarily to bring UK legislation into line with the European Council's new legislation and secondly to strengthen and close certain loopholes of the CDPA 1988. With the new Trade Marks Act the intention has been to make sure that the law meets more satisfactorily with industries and their commercial needs in today's competitive environment. Therefore, an owner of a registered trade mark under the 1994 Act is now given a broader protection, to allow legal action against anyone who uses, or tries to use, the same or similar mark on the same, or similar, goods as those for which the mark is registered.

Trade marks which make use of the 1994 Act through registration stand strongly as exclusive business assets which can be licensed, sold and bought and thereby have clear financial value.

Both of these current UK legislations—the CDPA 1988 and the Trade Marks Act 1994—are outlined in more detail in Chapters 4 and 5 coveing copyright, design right, patents, registered design and trade mark registration.

1.6 International copyright conventions

The UK is a member of several international conventions in the field of intellectual property rights, notably the Berne Convention of Literary and Artistic Works and the Universal Copyright Convention (UCC).

The Berne Copyright Convention 1886

Originating in 1886 and ratified in 1948 and 1971, the basic principles of this Convention are that, firstly 'Works originating in one of the member states must be given the same protection in each of the other member states as the latter grants to the works of its own nationals'. Secondly 'that such protection must not be conditional upon compliance with any formality'–it must be automatic.

Although this 'old' copyright Convention was established more than a century ago, it remains valid through ratifications to update the agreement. The growing realisation worldwide of the importance of intellectual property in today's business environment has seen a considerable increase of signatory countries to the Berne Convention, rising in membership from 70 to almost 120 states during the period 1992–96.

A full list of the 118 signatory countries as of August 1996 is found in Box 1.1. Every effort is made to ensure that the information given is accurate but changes to the list of membership states may take place without warning.

To confirm specific countries and their membership status contact the copyright enquiries department of a local Patent Office (see Address List at the end of this book).

Universal Copyright Convention 1952

This Convention was created as an international bridge between the Berne Convention members, the USA and USSR as it was known in the 1950s.

The standard of protection provided is lower than that of the Berne agreement, and the minimum terms of protection provided are shorter. The UCC does not allow automatic protection against membership countries, but instead limits the formalities that any country may demand. According to the Convention it is recommended that each published article carry the international © symbol, together with the year of first publication and the name of the copyright owner.

For the latest list of the 95 signatory membership states (as of August 1996) for the UCC agreement see Box 1.2. As for all international conventions the membership list may increase or change without warning. If necessary, contact the local copyright register to confirm possible changes.

Paris Convention for the Protection of Industrial Property

Originating in 1883 this international Convention has been revised and amended continuously, most recently in 1979. It is similar to the Berne Convention in that it states that amongst member countries the same

Box 1.1

Member states of the Berne Copyright Convention

(118 states as of August 1996)

Albania	Estonia	Luxembourg	Saint Vincent
Argentina	Fiji	Macedonia	and the
Australia	Finland	Madagascar	Grenadines
Austria	France	Malawi	Senegal
Bahamas	Gabon	Malaysia	Slovakia
Barbados	Gambia	Mali	Slovenia
Belgium	Georgia	Malta	South Africa
Benin	Germany	Mauritania	Spain
Bolivia	Ghana	Mauritius	Sri Lanka
Bosnia and	Greece	Mexico	Surinam
Herzegovina	Guinea	Monaco	Sweden
Brazil	Guinea–Bissau	Morocco	Switzerland
Bulgaria	Guyana	Namibia	Tanzania
Burkina Faso	Holy See	Netherlands	Thailand
Cameroon	Honduras	New Zealand	Togo
Canada	Hungary	Niger	Trinidad and
Central African	Iceland	Nigeria	Tobago
Republic	India	Norway	Tunisia
Chad	Ireland	Pakistan	Turkey
Chile	Isle of Man	Paraguay	Ukraine
China	Israel	Peru	United Kingdom
Colombia	Italy	Philippines	Uruguay
Congo	Jamaica	Poland	USA
Costa Rica	Japan	Portugal	Venezuela
Cote d'Ivoire	Kenya	Republic of	Yugoslavia
Croatia	Korea	Moldova	Zaire
Cyprus	Latvia	Romania	Zambia
Czech	Lebanon	Russian	Zimbabwe
Republic	Lesotho	Federation	
Denmark	Liberia	Rwanda	Source: The
Ecuador	Libya	Saints	Patent Office/
Egypt	Liechtenstein	Kitts/Nevis	Copyright
El Salvador	Lithuania	Saint Lucia	Directorate, UK

protection must be provided to nationals of other member states as granted to own nationals.

World Intellectual Property Organisation (WIPO)

As a result of the 1883 Paris Convention and the Berne Convention 1886 the specialist agency of the United Nations, known as WIPO, was

---

Box 1.2

Signatory states of the Universal Copyright Convention

(95 states as of August 1996)

Algeria	Republic	Liberia	Saint Vincent
Andorra	Denmark	Liechtenstein	and the
Argentina	Dominican	Luxembourg	Grenadines
Australia	Republic	Malawi	Saudi Arabia
Austria	Ecuador	Malta	Senegal
Bahamas	El Salvador	Mauritius	Slovakia
Bangladesh	Fiji	Mexico	Slovenia
Barbados	Finland	Monaco	Spain
Belarus	France	Morocco	Sri Lanka
Belgium	Germany	Netherlands	Sweden
Belize	Ghana	New Zealand	Switzerland
Bolivia	Greece	Nicaragua	Tajikistan
Bosnia and	Guatemala	Niger	Trinidad and
Herzegovina	Guinea	Nigeria	Tobago
Brazil	Haiti	Norway	Tunisia
Bulgaria	Holy See	Pakistan	Ukraine
Cambodia	Hungary	Panama	United Kingdom
Cameroon	Iceland	Paraguay	Uruguay
Canada	India	Peru	USA
Chile	Ireland	Philippines	Venezuela
China	Israel	Poland	Yugoslavia
Colombia	Italy	Portugal	Zambia
Costa Rica	Japan	Republic of	
Croatia	Kazakhstan	Korea	Source: The
Cuba	Kenya	Russian	Patent Office/
Cyprus	Laos	Federation	Copyright
Czech	Lebanon	Rwanda	Directorate, UK

---

established in 1974. The aim was to be able to co-ordinate the developments of international protection for all intellectual property categories (including inventions, industrial design and trade marks as well as literary and artistic works).

The World Trade Organisation (WTO)—TRIPs agreement 1995

In 1948, in the wake of the Second World War, 23 countries established the first General Agreement on Tariffs and Trade (GATT) dedicated to international economic co-operation. Over the years new and updated GATT agreements were developed with the main focus on tariffs and anti-dumping measures, involving a growing number of membership countries.

However, by the early 1980s it had become apparent that the General Agreement on Tariffs and Trade was no longer as relevant to the realities of world trade as it had been in the 1940s, partly due to the fact that the trade policy environment has deteriorated over the years. World trade has become far more complex and important, due to increasing globalisation of the world economy, international investment and a major growth in trade of services, all becoming more closely tied to the increase of world trade in products.

Whereas previous GATT rounds applied to trade in goods only, the new organisation established during the Uruguay Round negotiations—the World Trade Organisation (WTO)—covers trade both in goods and services as well as, for the first time, 'trade in ideas' or intellectual property.

The expansion and wider-ranging basis of issues covered by the new agreement was supported during negotiations, by the continuing rush of new member countries wishing to be included in what was generally seen as 'an anchor for development and an instrument of economic and trade reform'.

After long negotiations during the years 1986–93 to explore and clarify issues together with lengthy processes of consensus building, the Uruguay Round was finally signed by 123 countries in Marrakesh, April 1994 and came into force from January 1995 (see Box 1.3).

With the establishment of the WTO based in Geneva, significant changes have taken place. A much broader scope than GATT is now applied by the WTO in terms of commercial activity and trade policies. GATT was a set of rules which were applied on a provisional basis, with no institutional foundation—as opposed to the WTO which now exists as a permanent institution with a secretariat and a much wider council structure in place.

In connection to intellectual property, the specialised Council for Trade-Related Aspects of Intellectual Property Rights now exists on a permanent basis. Other sections of the new WTO structure which are of interest to the clothing and textile industry in other fields of inter-national trade include the Textiles Monitoring Body, the Committee on Rules of Origin, the Committee on Import Licensing and the Dispute Settlement Body.

Box 1.3

Member countries of the World Trade Organisation (WTO)

(123 countries as of July 1996)

Antigua/Barbuda	EC	Luxembourg	Saint Vincent
Argentina	Ecuador	Macau	and the
Australia	Egypt	Madagascar	Grenadines
Austria	El Salvador	Malawi	Senegal
Bahrain	Fiji	Malaysia	Sierra Leone
Bangladesh	Finland	Maldives	Singapore
Barbados	France	Mali	Slovak
Belgium	Gabon	Malta	Republic
Belize	Germany	Mauritania	Slovenia
Benin	Ghana	Mauritius	Solomon
Bolivia	Greece	Mexico	Islands
Botswana	Grenada	Morocco	South Africa
Brazil	Guatemala	Mozambique	Spain
Brunei	Guinea-Bissau	Myanmar	Sri Lanka
Darussalam	Guinea,	Namibia	Surinam
Burkina Faso	Republic of	Netherlands	Swaziland
Burundi	Guyana	New Zealand	Sweden
Cameroon	Haiti	Nicaragua	Switzerland
Canada	Honduras	Nigeria	Tanzania
Central African	Hong Kong	Norway	Thailand
Republic	Hungary	Pakistan	Togo
Chile	Iceland	Papua New	Trinidad and
Colombia	India	Guinea	Tobago
Costa Rica	Indonesia	Paraguay	Tunisia
Cote d'Ivoire	Ireland	Peru	Turkey
Cuba	Israel	Philippines	Uganda
Cyprus	Italy	Poland	United Arab
Czech	Jamaica	Portugal	Emirates
Republic	Japan	Qatar	United Kingdom
Denmark	Kenya	Romania	Uruguay
Djibouti	Korea	Rwanda	USA
Dominica	Kuwait	Saints	Venezuela
Dominican	Lesotho	Kitts/Nevis	Zambia
Republic	Liechtenstein	Saint Lucia	Zimbabwe

Observer governments (37) of the WTO

Albania	Bulgaria	Croatia	Kazakhstan
Algeria	Cambodia	Estonia	Kyrgyz Republic
Angola	Chad	Gambia	Latvia
Armenia	China	Georgia	Lithuania
Belarus	Congo	Jordan	Macedonia

Moldova	Panama	Sudan	Uzbekistan
Mongolia	Russian	Taipei,	Vanuatu
Nepal	Federation	Chinese	Vietnam
Niger	Saudi Arabia	Tonga	Zaire
Oman	Seychelles	Ukraine	

Sections in the WTO agreement which deal with the Trade-Related Aspects of Intellectual Property Rights—known as the TRIPs agreement—along with other general developments and implications for the textile and clothing industries are covered in further detail in Chapter 8.

This chapter has examined and outlined the origin and major developments over the last 400 years of intellectual property protection, from specifically targeted copyright law towards the different categories of protection in the 20th century through copyright, patents, registered design and trade marks. Each type of protection offers specific protection rights for specific categories of products—ranging from original artistic work to purely functional inventive products. In addition to the UK legislation, new ongoing developments towards international agreements and European legislation help to facilitate the increasing needs of international business operations.

The following chapters will continue to look more closely at each of the protection types available to the British clothing industry and how to go about protecting designs and/or trade marks effectively whilst the book's later chapters deal with European and international developments.

2

WHY BE CONCERNED WITH DESIGN PROTECTION?

2.1 Design and economic success

The creation and development of new innovative products together with the encouragement and growth of commerce is essential to the economic well-being of a nation's economy which is part of today's competitive market-place. To achieve these advances depends not only on the ingenuity of designers and engineers, but includes the investment necessary to develop new ideas and market them effectively. Intellectual property rights, which give legal recognition to the concept of intangible properties, provide the proprietor with a means of preventing other people from exploiting his property thereby safeguarding the investment made in new products.

In business it has become increasingly important for fashion companies to protect current and future business opportunities when marketing new innovative product ranges. When developing an original fashion range be it under a new or already established trade mark a company will have made considerable investments through time spent on developing the range and considerable research in the field of textiles, style trends, projected market segments, customer and pricing strategies. Before the final garment range is launched, products will have undergone various stages of creative design input, prototype development and selection processes. The purpose being to try and ensure the garments not only appeal to the projected target customer and retail sectors but also achieve sufficient financial returns through sales which will cover the creative investments and initial layout and altogether make the range profitable and competitive.

By reviewing the subject in a business context intellectual property protection can be regarded, metaphorically, as separate building blocks from which a wall can be built protecting the business and its investment.[11] This wall will allow the business a space within which to develop products which can achieve maximum market success and financial gain through investment. Also, it should be noted that the most efficient business protection does not necessarily occur from *one* major innovation. Rather than launching a design concept which is completely new and untested in the market-place and which involves a high risk business strategy a series of small advances may be more profitable and increase a company's business strength in the long run by interlocking the developments as they emerge.

In relation to the growing importance of pan-European and international business through export, intellectual property likewise plays a crucial part. Superior design is an important instrument for European industries in their competition with industries from Third World countries which offer lower production costs. It is the design which, in many cases, is decisive for the commercial success of products thus allowing European enterprises investing heavily in development of designs to prosper.[1]

The reason why a proprietor should be concerned with protecting intellectual property was summed up perfectly in a short statement by the High Court: 'What is worth copying, is worth protecting'. The financial business value of a well executed and innovative design be it individual garments or entire ranges should never be underestimated. During the research and product development stages for fashion industries, a number of complex elements such as colour, shape, aesthetics, fashion trends as well as functional aspects are assessed and combined through the creative human intellect in a way which can be highly influential on the designs success in terms of being able to make or break a product's sales appeal and ultimately ensure a strong competitive advantage towards designs from business competitors.

It is also interesting to notice that since the late 1980s a growing number of public companies view brand names as a company asset and include the brand value on their balance sheet. Such brand valuations include for example 'Guinness' which on the first financial brand assessment was valued at £1.7 billion. Viewed as a financial asset, it becomes quite obvious that designers and company managers should take a keen interest in making sure that the intellectual property and its ownership is effectively and sufficient protected.

2.2 Copying and the fashion industry

The saying that 'imitation is the sincerest form of flattery' has for many years been used as an excuse by clothing companies trying to legitimise their copying.

As an example of how widespread copying and design 'interpretations' are in the fashion industry, it is interesting to note the following: through the author's conversation with a number of people working in various cross-sections of the clothing industry (at a postgraduate reunion meeting held in 1995 for product development managers at a leading UK design faculty), it appeared that already within the first year spent in the fashion industry it was the rule rather than the exception to have experienced some form of contact with direct copying and design interpretations—more commonly referred to as the 'rip-off'—from a competitor's design. The reasons behind copying varied from increasing market share in a competitive business to a cost-cutting exercise to reduce the cost of research and development stages for products.

The problem with plagiarism is that reproduction of design products does not require sophisticated know-how, creative skills or cost-consuming R&D. It is therefore important that appropriate measures, such as effective legal protection, exist to deal with design piracy to protect the interests of design investing companies.[1]

However, some fashion companies have established a reputation for spotting upcoming trends amongst *haute couture* fashion. Copying or using them as a basis for interpretation can mean an R&D lead time from start to finish of only six weeks before the copy garments are retailing to customers and, importantly, at a fraction of the original price.

To achieve a high street retail price of less than £40 for a garment rather than the couture price of £2,500, design alterations must take place. Typical changes include using a cheaper fabric with similar appearance to the original material, removing unnecessary lining, pockets, trimming detail and seam constructions, as well as engineering cheaper production methods and trying to limit the overall material consumption of the new copy as much as possible. An example of this type of plagiarism is shown in Figure 2.1, comparing the original with a copy design.

Some design copying companies will argue that for brands such as Chanel, Gucci, Hermes or Versace, the customer only wants the label and does not care about cheap copies. Nevertheless companies like Chanel,

FROM £2,500 . . .   . . . TO £34.99

Figure 2.1 Copy of a couture dress (reproduced with the permission of Solo Syndication Ltd, © 1993 The Daily Mail)

Vuitton and Cartier each initiate 2,000 actions a year, spending in the region of US$7 million each year, to protect investments made in creating prestige brand labels.

A common view regarding design plagiarism, held by a large proportion of designers and companies involved in the development and marketing of original and innovative design products can be illustrated by the Italian designer of furniture, Mario Bellini. In the journal *Design* he expressed his viewpoint on the subject of plagiarism concisely: 'What makes me happy is when I am imitated in a rather clever way, that is the right way . . . [e.g. an original simple concept which someone develops further through their imitation] . . . But if someone copies the details, I feel robbed of money and of my inventive rights' (January 1992).

The acute feeling of theft experienced by the creator and/or the rights owner in cases of illegal copying may be understood more clearly when viewing the parameters involved in design. The process of developing and executing original and innovative design is not just a question of choosing or applying a range of 'finishing touches'. Across industries, other than fashion, producing successful industrial design includes the following general elements which require consideration through R&D stages:

- materials
- appearance
- product/material safety
- existing design products
- target customer and market
- corporate business strategy
- quality required
- price level
- functional performance
- ergonomics
- product maintenance
- environmental factors
- durability/flexibility/reliability
- packaging/presentation
- marketing needs
- production methods and volume
- cost-effective aspects
- lead time and time restriction.

The priority and importance of design elements will of course vary depending on the product, customer and business environment.

2.3 Brand imitation

The production of imitation goods selling at a fraction of the original product's price has become one of the boom industries in recent years. The huge scale of the problem has consistently been reported through the 1990s both in national and international newspapers and trade journals. In overall terms it is estimated that there are 10 or 20 times more copies of prestige brand articles on sale than are produced by the legitimate owners of the trade mark.

Table 2.1 shows examples of the considerable price difference between well established brand names compared to the prices required for illegal imitation goods which are meant to look exactly like 'the real thing' at first glance. The vast majority of pirate clothing is notoriously known for severe failure in quality, performance and durability and will quickly show the signs of product failure during wash and wear. Under circumstances where customers are aware of having purchased an imitation product, some may argue that the general quality expectations are likely to be low and any brand perception damage to be limited. However, in the instance of goods being bought and believed to be the true brand, i.e. they are imitated so closely as to being indistinguishable to the original brand and possibly even sold at the same price as the original product, the damage resulting from poor quality and faulty goods will be much greater. To re-establish the consumer's brand loyalty in such instances may prove very difficult.

The high level of counterfeiting experienced by established trade marks has in some instances led companies to bring in their own permanent team of detectives to track down suppliers of imitation clothing. One such firm producing legendary branded casual wear found in the early 1990s that they were losing around £250,000 every year through

Table 2.1 Price levels of brand imitations: Original products vs. brand copies

	Original brand (£)	Imitation copies (£)
T-shirts with designer logo	25–30	5–8
Men's shirts, e.g. Armani, Pringle, Hugo Boss	35–70	10–12
Jackets such as Naf Naf, Fila, Lacoste	50–80	15–25
Branded jeans/denim wear, e.g. Levi 501	40–50	10–18

counterfeit imitations. At this serious level of infringement the company felt that severe action *had* to be taken to protect the trade mark and designs. A business news bulletin was published in several trade journals clearly stating the company's actions of employing permanent investigators to combat counterfeit products, reinforcing the message and making potential counterfeiters think twice before producing any imitations of the brand.

Reports in recent years by the Trading Standards Association and the Anti-Counterfeiting Group have found a dramatic overall increase in counterfeiting since 1990 which is believed to be worth as much as

Figure 2.2 Pirate imitations (b) compared to the original branded products (a) (Reproduced with the permission of APACS (Administration) Ltd, © 1990)

£1 billion a year. With technological development and improvements, quality levels of 'pirate' products have increased, in single cases resulting in investigators being unable to tell the difference between clothing products made by the original manufacturer and the fake goods.

The US shoe and clothing manufacturer Converse Inc.—the maker of 520 million pairs of authentic Chuck Taylor All Star sneakers since 1917—confirms this problem: 'Copies are extremely good. So good, that sometimes the only difference between authentic and fake, is the much cheaper price of the counterfeit shoe' (*The Times*, 1993).

The reaction from the internationally known sports shoe brand was to join the battle against counterfeiters with an advertisement campaign which has appeared in the trade press across Europe since the early 1990s. The stark warning has been 'Rip Us Off, Go To Jail'. The aim is to protect its famous Chuck Taylor All Star shoe which in 1993 made it on to the New York catwalks, achieving fashion status and selling some 20 million pairs over a period of two years.

The threat of jail sentences is becoming actual fact, as UK legislation takes the stance that counterfeiting is a serious crime. One of the earlier cases resulting in a UK prison sentence in relation to the production of fake brand clothing took place during October 1993—initiated and successfully won by the company Naf Naf. The legal outcome was for the defendant to receive a sentence of 12 months' imprisonment.

2.4 The importance of trade marks and brand loyalty

The following contribution from the independent retailer 'Strawberry Fields' illustrates the importance of trade marks and brand names not only to customers but indeed to the retailer when selling fashion-led product ranges. In recent years the majority of multiple retail chains have been focused on increasing their market share of price competitive, own-brand merchandise. However, department stores and fashion-led independents are rapidly discovering the financial magnitude of high profile brands particularly at the design-led quality end of the children's wear market. Reports from recent trade exhibitions such as 'Premier Children's Wear' confirm that collections produced under designer brands such as Chevignon, Paul Smith, Guess, Levis for Kids and Sonia Rykiel are selling particularly well to the market range of 8–14 year olds.

CASE STUDY

Viewpoint of an independent retailer by Danielle Metzstein, Proprietor, Strawberry Fields (Glasgow)

Strawberry Fields has been trading in Glasgow since 1978 specialising in up-market continental brands for kids. Within the children's wear sector brand loyalty is led by parents until the child reaches eight years whereafter the brand selection and preference is led by the child.

In comparison with the 1980s with its high consumer spending, customers in the 1990s are showing much greater brand loyalty which means that it is becoming increasingly difficult to sell a less known brand that is not supported by substantial advertising and marketing to 'win over' the customer and in many cases unknown brands end up being ignored despite excellent design and quality.

Designer fashion seems to be a fairly new phenomenon at high street level and in recent years many multiple retailers have acknowledged the importance and added value of designer branding compared to their own high street brand names with a large number of UK multiples now working closely with well-known designers to launch stronger design-led ranges.

For children's wear one way of trying to attract customers to an unknown brand and achieve consumer loyalty is to introduce an unknown brand in the baby range where a design might appeal regardless of name and then slowly extend the new trade mark into older age categories. Alternatively, if customers display reluctance to buying unknown brands the only option may be to sell the garments in the major sales thereby losing substantial profit margin. Once customers realise the quality and performance of the previously unknown brand they may return in the new season to buy the trade mark at full price, once they are convinced of the brand qualities.

For certain items such as jeans and trainers, branding is of paramount importance as it is practically impossible if you are a fashion shop to sell jeans that are not named with a well-known trade mark or that send out a recognisable signal in the form of a label or a specially engraved button. This is invading almost all items of clothing in one form or another, even though the branding may not be visible during wear but more clearly incorporated into the design, e.g. Calvin Klein men's underpants which have the name woven into the waistband or socks which sport a tiny named label such as Armani. Consistency of branding is important for other items such as caps, scarves, sunglasses, and bags quite apart from the big items of clothing such as sweaters and sweatshirts.

The phenomenon is not confined to the adult world of fashion but is becoming of increasing prevalence in the world of children's fashions. When I first started in the business in 1978, in retrospect, to be successful, it was sufficient to source continental clothes, mainly from France. The fabrics that were used were of a much higher quality than in Britain, and the colour palette did not confine itself to navy, brown or bottle green with grey reserved for school colours, while babies were dressed exclusively in sky, rose and lemon! It almost seemed the rule that all girl babies had to wear very short frilly clothes to show frilly knickers.

It is difficult to know in retrospect the reasons why Scotland or perhaps Britain was so lagging behind and seemed stuck in a 1950s mode. But with the opening of my shop 'Strawberry Fields—Clothes for Kids' it was a real pleasure to introduce good clear design in sharp colours including black and much darker shades for babies. In a fashion shop back then it was sufficient that the clothes were from the Continent, that seemed to give them enough cachet to sell successfully. At that time adult clothes were very exciting and daring. There was a significant difference between them and children's clothes.

Slowly, over the years, children's clothes have become very like their adult counterparts, sometimes appearing a season later and now, due to the large number of designers who bring out a junior range, they appear simultaneously. In the 1980s there were a number of designers of children's clothes who were very avant-garde and who even seemed to predate fashions that came later in the adult market once the design's popularity had been tested in the children's wear sector.

In the 1980s numerous new brand names appeared and were supported by customers' high spending and reduced concern with brand name loyalty, quality and durability requirements compared to the 1990s consciousness for quality and value.

However, on the subject of the strength of brand names some very strong brands of the 1980s seem to have been victims of their own success. Although phenomenally successful in branded fashion sectors, they spawned many imitators until retail outlets were full of imitations and the original trade mark was no longer fashionable but became quite down-market. Examples of this trend have in the past included Lacoste with its crocodile logo and Naf Naf whose clothes were illegally copied on a large scale.

Today alongside the unknown brands, due to world advertising and media interest, there are now brand names that sell well in the shop almost regardless of design or garment construction. As long as they have the right label that can be readily identified they have become desirable products, e.g. Armani, Versace, Moschino, Calvin Klein, Ralph Lauren, DKNY. They seem to be a response to a personality cult or the image of a certain lifestyle. Ralph Lauren in particular epitomises this trend without the need to use the name directly on clothing but instead making use of a small embroidered emblem of a polo player on his horse. This little logo is so well recognised and valued by customers, that it can sell anything and commands great respect.

This, however, makes it increasingly difficult to promote any new designers and new brands that do not have a recognised name or a big advertising campaign backing them. Most people look at the label first and the garment second. Whether this is a lasting situation or if we have come to the apogee of brand-led buying and selling is difficult to gauge. But certainly the brand name loyalty of today's customer has reached an ultimate level of importance.

2.5 Design copying—a cost reduction strategy

The number of design and copyright disputes increased considerably during the recession period of the early 1990s, with some multiple retailers turning a blind eye to design infringement. The business response in such instances has been to try and maintain profitability during times of low consumer spending and reduced turnover by increasing the level of profit earned per unit.

In some instances this has resulted in large retailers cancelling orders and reproducing garments overseas using cheaper materials in order to cut costs. Rather than paying the comparatively higher prices of UK suppliers, cost-saving short cuts may be pursued to improve the profit margin on garments. As an example a multiple retailer can instead go to the Far East or other low-cost countries, with a sample garment and ask manufacturers there to copy it in the knowledge that small suppliers often cannot afford to sustain legal action.

EXAMPLE

The supplier and retail multiples

Whilst working with a smaller London-based children's wear company supplying major multiple retail chains — several instances were encountered where either a textile design or a complete dress design, created by the design company but not ordered by the retailer, would appear in a number of stores a couple of months after the buying season, retailing at a considerably lower price point than could have been achieved by the original London supplier.

Never having had to deal with this situation or taken time to understand the framework of intellectual property rights and legislation, both management and the in-house children's wear designer found themselves on very uncertain ground. Apart from the lost orders and sales revenue, there was a high level of general upset from having the business asset of creative designs stolen from the collection. Should the children's wear company take a clear stand against the infringement of their designs and face the possibility of a major dispute with the retail chain?

Following discussions between sales and design managers it was concluded that, due to the large amount of orders placed by the same retail organisation involving other designs, the decision was made to ignore the infringement, partly to avoid jeopardising existing and future business contracts and partly due to the risk of excessive costs if pursuing the matter legally.

Points of question for this infringement case

Did the children's wear supplier really take the best decision for the business? Without the involvement or contribution of anyone familiar with intellectual property rights, was the decision of no action instead a reflection of managers becoming mentally paralysed by the mere thought of legal complexities? In trying not to damage current and other future orders from this major account, will the 'no action' policy ensure that copying by the same retailer does not happen again—possibly on an even larger scale?

It may be argued that by tolerating design copying, the children's wear company in fact did the complete opposite of taking care of their business interest, indeed they exposed themselves to loss of future business contracts by ending up being viewed by the retail chain as a 'design greenhouse' where innovative designs are developed and minor trial orders are placed. However, once the design then proves successful through the small trial order, any major repeat orders are placed overseas where lower costs will allow the retailer higher profit margins and the original children's wear supplier loses out on large future business contracts.

Another option which was also not investigated by the design company was the extent of the retail chain or buyer's direct involvement with the design copying; did the retail chain knowingly procure the manufacture and/or purchase and/or importation of the copies to be sold in the UK shops or was any third party responsible for copying and selling the design to the retail chain?

3

INTELLECTUAL PROPERTY AND OWNERSHIP

3.1 Categories of intellectual property rights

When looking at the structure of intellectual property (IP) protection available under the UK legal system it is worth keeping in mind that the law applies to a vast range of industries and types of products—ranging from technological inventions, highly artistic 'one-of-a-kind' objects through to mass-produced designs. This is one of the reasons why the legal field is often found to be highly complex as it tries to satisfy the diverse needs of very different industries and individual requirements.

When dealing with fashion and textiles it is also the case that during design and development stages different types of intellectual property rights can apply. For example automatic copyright exists in the design document as soon as the design is drawn on paper (or in another tangible form), provided the work is *original*. In addition the design of the garment itself may be protected by automatic design right, 'registered design protection' or 'registered trade mark protection' thereby strengthening the legal protection of the design in its three-dimensional form.

On the subject of intellectual property which a company or individual wishes to commercially exploit to protect against copying, passing off or unfair competition, there are generally two main categories under which protection can be achieved for original works:

- *Statutory rights.* Automatically come into effect from the moment of creation, when the original work is first drawn or outlined in a tangible design document be it on paper or a computer representation. These rights cover specific areas and types of design, and exist in the UK by 'copyright' or 'design right'. The latter category was introduced into English law with the latest legislation CDPA 1988, in order to meet the needs of industry working with design for commercial production on a larger scale.

- *Registered rights.* Exist in the form of 'patent', 'registered design' and 'registered trade mark' protection and are based on monopoly rights as opposed to control of copyright-based ownership rights. By nature these protection types involve certain formalities including time and cost factors in relation to publication of the design or invention.

  Although registered rights do not guarantee absolute protection, official registration will in most cases be sufficient in a court of law without further proof necessary for the time of creation/existence and publication. When it comes to upholding and protecting the registered IP rights, this responsibility remains with the registration holder.

In the United Kingdom the Patent Office is responsible for granting patents, registered designs and registered trade marks.

The above rights granted either by statute or registration under UK law are effective only in the UK. Protecting one's design, trade mark or other intellectual property abroad will often depend on the protection available from individual countries' legal systems and laws. In many cases countries will be signatory to one of the international agreements such as the Berne Convention, Universal Copyright Convention or the TRIPs agreement under the World Trade Organisation.

On a European level new legislation is developing specifically for industrial design with the Community design registration which will help to protect rights within the EU Member States as well as making it easier to obtain the IP rights for design protection. Existing EU legislation already makes it possible to register a European trade mark, achieving IP rights throughout the EU via a single application to the European trade marks registry—OHIM.

3.2 Premature disclosure

A common error, made through the unfamiliarity or newness of working with registered protection for a novel/original work be it for patents or more commonly used registered designs is to disclose an invention or design prematurely. This is simply because one precondition to allowing an application for a patent or registered design is that the work must not in any way have been publicised prior to filing the registration application.

Discussing or showing the work *before* filing an application to anyone who is not under a legal obligation to keep all information confidential via contract or by the nature of the relationship with them (e.g. colleagues within the same company) constitutes a 'prior publication' and will automatically bar the application for a patent or registered design.[11]

When working with intellectual property, especially where maximum commercial exploitation is to be pursued via registered protection, one should therefore exercise vigilance and the necessary care not to make the work available or disclose it to the public in any way whatsoever. To avoid unnecessary constraints some of the select exceptions which do exist to allow pre-disclosure include:

- *Confidential disclosure* is accepted when the parties involved are all bound by an agreement of confidentiality.
- *Professional advice* e.g. from one's own patent agent, personal legal adviser or solicitor who will need to know invention details and the work in order to advise. In such circumstances the professional adviser has a legal duty of confidentiality, and the information will therefore not be classified as premature disclosure.
- *Certified display* allows a design to be displayed at an exhibition *provided* this is certified by the Department of Trade and Industry prior to filing an application for registration, as long as the application is made within six months of the opening of the exhibition.[7]

The requirement for no premature disclosure in advance of obtaining registered protection rights should be seen as a positive measure in the interest of the creator/owner. It is not a mere obstacle to ensure application fees are paid to the official registration source. In the case of trade exhibitions it will clearly help the creator to have filed the application and obtained registration acknowledgement, should competitors be found to be copying or infringing other rights, the rightful owner will then have the proof of the official registration number to support an ownership claim. Hence, when considering the option of registration to protect an original and novel work caution must be exercised to avoid pre-empting one's qualification by disregarding general conditions and requirements allowing applications to be filed. Refer to Chapter 5 which outlines the specific requirements for IP categories of patents and design registrations.

Once an application has been filed with the Patent Office for registration of an invention or design, publication can take place at *any* time including the intermediate period of time when the granting of the registration is being considered. Hence, display or disclosure will not have to wait the full period it takes to process an application and until the registration is granted.

3.3 Search of existing concepts and designs

Another quite common error according to the Patent Office is for companies and individuals to become single-minded about their ideas and new concepts and fail to research other existing concepts or ideas already developed and registered or available in the market-place, i.e. from competitors. Instead they have gone ahead and invested heavily in money, time and R&D activities, only to find that the invention, design or trade mark is not 'new' at all but is already being used by another company. It can therefore be very worthwhile to carry out a preliminary search via the Patent Office database or search agencies to establish the latest developments both technically and commercially. Should the concept already exist, it may be possible to analyse the existing registration and propose a more sophisticated and far superior solution to the problem being tackled. This approach, of inventing or developing around a prior concept, is often found by the Patent Office to be the way in which major industrial companies advance their interests whilst at the same time avoiding wasting resources in 'redeveloping' and creating concepts already in existence.[11]

For a fee, a search can be carried out by the Patent Office, Design Registry or Trade Mark Registry. The search will help to determine whether a identical or highly similar work be it an invention, a registered design or trade mark has already been registered although the search may only be viewed as a 'snapshot' because new concepts are being filed and registered all the time. As a rough guide the cost involved in a registered design search is in the range of £25. The type of information recorded and available for such searches is listed in Box 3.1. Note that public access is not given to inspect actual three-dimensional representations of the registered designs but copies of the recorded information concerning specific registrations can be obtained.

However, it is not only registered designs, trade marks or patents held by the Patent Office, Design Registry and Trade Mark Registry which allow for searching. In addition a number of independent search agencies have been established throughout the UK with extensive databases and search facilities for various intellectual property categories.

One such search agency is the Manchester based 'Clothing Namecheck'. Launched by solicitors Linder Myers it specialises in checking against unregistered clothing trade marks from a database of over 30,000 brand names against a charge of approximately £50. The benefit

---

Box 3.1

Information available for search of registered designs

1. Names and addresses of the proprietors.
2. The statement of article.
3. Date of the issue or grant of the Certificate of Registration.
4. Filing date of the application.
5. Any 'priority date' claimed from a previous overseas filing.
6. The number(s) of any earlier designs with which the design is associated.
7. Notices of licences, assignments or other documents affecting the design.
8. Notices of extensions (if any) of the original period of protection.

Source: The Patent Office,UK[5]

---

of the search is to identify brands not widely known or used by smaller companies which may only be trading locally or in certain regions of the country. Because of the small-scale use of the trade mark the local company may not wish to formally register the brand. But having traded and become known under the unregistered trade mark the company could claim rights in the brand which might make it impossible for another company to obtain the trade mark through registration or enabling the first user to prevent another company using a similar brand.

Therefore when trying to register a trade mark it is important to carry out substantial searches both of other registered as well as unregistered trade marks, to avoid brand disputes from companies or individuals claiming earlier use and ownership of the name. Such disputes could prove particularly costly if product ranges have already been developed and produced with the trade mark, and the claimant is unwilling to sell the ownership rights or reach a settlement.

3.4 Ownership

Intellectual ownership rights whether they concern copyright, patents, registered designs or trade marks, are all regarded as business property which can be bought, sold or licensed, like any other standard commodity.[6] If an invention or design is produced as a result of employment with a company, ownership and obligation of confidentiality will normally be owed to the commissioner or employer. However, employment contracts specifying shared or other types of ownership can be drawn up between the employer and employee which *will* be legally binding.

In instances where an original innovation is of outstanding value or benefit to the employer, it is possible the employee may be in a position to benefit from receiving compensation which is over and above his normal remuneration, provided the employment contract clearly specifies such arrangements. Quite complex legal factors can be involved in this aspect of intellectual property, and individuals should therefore seek *specific professional advice* to clarify any doubt or questions regarding the exact ownership rights of the intellectual property. In the case of employed designers or inventors developing work in their own time, with their own resources and even in their own home, it *could* be assumed that ownership automatically belongs to the creator. However, this may or may not be so, depending on the individual contract of employment and its nature.[11]

Alternatively, a company may buy designs from an outside source, be it textiles, garments, trade mark artwork or similar. In these situations it is equally important to specify the exact ownership of the work created by the external source.

Typical examples of the various ownership options generally applied in the textile industry are shown in the example opposite.

3.5 Enforcing ownership

Having achieved a patent, registered design or registered trade mark, it should be highlighted that while it will be much easier to prove intellectual ownership rights, official registration does *not* automatically secure the owner against infringements or ensure that the state will somehow 'police' the owner's rights. At all times it will be the responsibility of the registered owner to ensure that his interests and rights are protected.

The clear guidelines are that 'The law provides the necessary machinery, but it is the property owner's own responsibility to use that machinery for his purpose'.[11]

Enforcing one's rights and dealing with various types of copying and passing off are covered in more detail throughout Chapter 6.

EXAMPLE

Ownership of a textile design

A clothing company is sourcing fabric for its next collection of garments and buys fabric from a textile manufacturer as:

Stock fabric—*the material is part of the textile manufacturer's own range which is sold to various clothing producers without granting any exclusive rights. Ownership of the fabric design remains with the textile manufacturer.*

Exclusive rights—*the design company may buy the design with exclusive supply rights for a specific clothing sector (i.e. evening wear) or a market (i.e. the UK or EU countries) to avoid competitors producing garments in the same fabric. In this instance it is important to clarify and confirm points such as:*

- *do exclusive supply rights include all or only selected colourways of the design, without signing over the actual ownership right or licence of the design?*
- *time restrictions. Are the exclusive rights limited to a specific season?*
- *minimum order quantity (specified per order or over a period of time). The supplier will often specify this to cover the R&D costs of the design.*
- *has the same fabric more recently been sold to competitors or the same target market? As fabric is often sold through more than one agent and at various trade exhibitions, it may be necessary to consult central sales records for the design to confirm this.*

Commissioned textile design—*a number of ownership disputes have occurred in this field when a company request designs by commission or through freelance work. The major point being that although the commissioning company may specify various details or guidelines, does the ownership in fact belong to the company/commissioner or to the individuals/organisations that carry out the creative work through drawings or design samples and swatches? As a general guideline, the ownership of design commissions will belong to the person commissioning the design.*

However, when working with commission agreements, be it to issue or to accept a design commission, it is of ultimate importance that all parties involved specify and agree to the full extent of the commission including the aspects of the commission purpose/application, duration and the scale of commercial exploitation. These factors should then be reflected in the commission's payment terms, which may be one single and final payment for the work created. Alternatively, it may be part of the agreed commission contract that a initial smaller payment is made on completing the design, followed by sales-linked commission in which case the commissioned creator will continue to benefit from the sales of a successful design.

3.6 Marking articles

Marking articles is one way of making sure that competitors are aware of the intellectual ownership being claimed on a product. Though such marking is not legally required in the UK, proprietors should be aware that in proceedings concerning infringement of registered designs, damages may not be awarded against a defendant who can prove beyond reasonable doubt that there was no grounds to suppose the design was registered. This point makes it only logical to ensure registered rights are clearly marked on the product.

When marking articles, it is not sufficient to simply use the word 'registered' or a similar abbreviation, the marking must include the registration number.[5]

This point of registration marking is often misinterpreted or confused with the issue 'Does that mean that although a design may be published at any time after an application has been filed with the registration authorities, in reality it is not possible to mark the products until the registration number is issued at a later date, when the application has been fully processed?' The answer is 'No'.

When the registration application is filed the official registry will issue an application reference number as a receipt. This number is synonymous with the final registration number. Once the application has been processed and is successful in obtaining registration the Patent Office—or in cases of design, the Design Registry—will issue the official 'Certificate of Registration' which will carry the registration number identical to the initial application number.

Therefore, in the interim period between filing an application and achieving registration, the product *can* be published and clearly marked to indicate ownership including the pending registration. It should, however, be quite clearly stated that the registration is *pending* as opposed to having obtained the registration due to the fact that it is an offence to mark articles as registered when they are not or when the registration has lapsed or expired.

Examples of how the product can be marked, depending on the type of intellectual property, include the following:

- For *registered designs*: 'Pending Design Reg. UK12345' and once registration is obtained 'Design Reg. UK12345'.

- In the case of a new **trade mark** the product can be marked for example as: 'HIGHNESS™' until the brand name is officially accepted and registered. Thereafter the marking would simply be 'HIGHNESS®'.
- **Patents** which do not apply very often to fashion and textile products: the product marking between date of application and registration would typically be: 'Pending Pat. No. 87654321' or 'Pat. Pending'.

Intellectual property such as design drawings or other material covered by *automatic copyright*, can be marked with the international © mark followed by the name of the copyright owner and year of publication.

For clothing and textile products intellectual ownership marks will typically include one of the following:

- sew-in label stating the ownership type and registration number where applicable;
- swing tickets, packaging or display material with printed ownership information;
- for fabric sold by the metre ownership details may be printed along the selvedge edge of each roll of material.

Note, that although copyright marking is not required by law in the UK, in the case of infringement proceedings it may support the owner's case considerably, while in certain countries it will be part of the legal requirement that goods are clearly marked with any ownership claim.

4

INTELLECTUAL PROPERTY LEGISLATION AND IP CATEGORIES IN THE UK

Before the introduction of the latest legislation—the Copyright, Designs and Patents Act (CDPA) 1988—automatic protection rights for clothing relied on the Copyright Act of 1956. The earlier legislation allowed limited protection of original drawings, sketches and works of artistic craftsmanship created by independent skills but was inadequate for the needs of the fashion industry.

Because the copyright protection relating to textiles and clothing primarily protected two-dimensional sketches, design drawings, pattern blocks and original surface decoration, these were viewed as artistic works even though they may have lacked artistic merit. However, the actual (three-dimensional) garment had, in most cases, no protection of its own, but depended purely on the design documents relating to the product. Any legal claim would therefore be for the infringement of the copyright in the *drawings*, not for the actual garments. Furthermore, the design documents supporting any claim of garment copying was required to show *all* details incorporated in the production garments. The obvious problem of the fashion industry was that during the development stages of garments, it is not unusual for a design to undergo several changes and alterations from the initial drawing to the finished production sample. Therefore the final pre-production sample or engineered production garment itself would often look quite different to the first design drawing. Hence, under the 1956 Copyright Act the original drawing would in many instances not show sufficient or correct design details to prove copyright ownership.

Copyright protection of the garment itself *could* nevertheless be achieved under the 1956 Act, if 'artistic craftsmanship' was involved and the design was produced industrially in quantities of 'less than 50 units'. Although in reality, the description of 'original work' gave no specification details for the quality of work and much argument raged as to the 'minimum requirement' of artistic merit required to claim copyright for works of artistic craftsmanship. Therefore for the purpose of fashion garments which more often than not were being produced on a larger scale than 50 units, the 'original work' protection rarely had useful applications for fashion companies.

For a number of years the diverse nature of the various types of intellectual property proved problematic and finally a new law was introduced. With the new CDPA 1988, several dramatic changes were introduced which also took into consideration the particular needs of the fashion industry. Whereas an invention in any industry may be the fruit of several years' work, research and development, a fashion designer may produce a couple of hundred designs in a year. This aspect of different needs for different industries had for years remained a stumbling block in providing effective and practical design protection for the clothing industry.

A notable change to fashion industries in the 1988 Act was the addition of a statutory 'design right' which was added to copyright protection. The major difference was that general protection was now given directly to the product design in its three-dimensional format (therefore *not* relying purely on two-dimensional material such as drawings) and secondly giving the creator rights against unauthorised copying of the design for a certain period of time.

Other changes included extending the registered design protection from 15 years to a possible 25 years from the date of registration. And whereas the proprietor of a registered design previously had to prove that an alleged infringer had copied the original design, this requirement was discontinued by the new law by way of making registered designs monopoly-based. Instead, the legal requirement is now that it is the accused counterfeit party who must prove how the alleged infringing design has been created and that they have not made an article to the registered design.

The various lengths of time that different types of intellectual property can be protected for in the UK are shown in Figure 4.1. To clarify the specific details and different groups of intellectual property protection Chapters 4 and 5 will describe the legislative mechanics to allow businesses—and individuals—to incorporate these protection measures within the daily business operations.

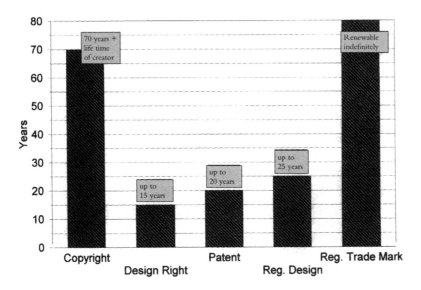

Figure 4.1 Maximum duration of IP protection: intellectual property types in the UK

This chapter begins by looking at the two types of automatic/statutory protection available in the United Kingdom: copyright and design right. Registered IP protection for the UK is covered in Chapter 5 with patents, registered design and registered trade marks.

4.1 Copyright

The purpose of copyright protection is to prevent the reproduction of a work—be it completely or in part—without the permission of the creator/owner. This also includes reproductions which involve adaptions. Copyright arises automatically as soon as a work takes some form from which it can be reproduced (including storage in a computer). No action or official acknowledgement of the work is necessary to establish, secure or maintain copyright.

It is, however, advisable to mark the work, as a warning to others, with the standard copyright formula:

© + **name of the copyright owner + year of first publication.**

In the UK such copyright marking is not required by law but will, in a legal dispute, clearly strengthen the copyright holder's claim of ownership. Also, under the Universal Copyright Convention, to which the UK is a signatory, works are in fact required to be marked with the © details as listed above, if they are to benefit from the international Convention in other membership countries.

Copyright protection gives rights to the creators of certain kinds of material so that control can be exercised over the various ways in which their material may be exploited and covers copying, adapting, publishing, performing and broadcasting. The main categories of material protected by copyright include: original literary, dramatic, musical and *artistic works*, published editions of works, sound recordings, films and broadcasts. Note that a name or title generally has no copyright protection in itself unless it is artistically represented.[6]

Duration of copyright protection

The copyright protection of original and artistic work lasts for the lifetime of the author plus a further 70 years, both in the case of published and unpublished work. In instances where artistic works are published and exploited as industrially produced articles, the owner's copyright will last for 25 years and thereafter the scope of protection is reduced. This shorter copyright term is based on the standard assumption that the larger quantities from industrial processes will recover possible investment costs faster than works produced in limited quantities.

Copyright and industrial articles

The general rule for design products being viewed as 'industrial design' is linked to the '50 rule' quantity—when designs are reproduced in larger quantities than 50. And although copyright may protect the *drawing* of an industrial design, it does not generally protect the industrial article (in the three-dimensional format). Neither will the copyright protect against the manufacture of articles made up from a design drawing unless they qualify as works of artistic craftsmanship.[6] In cases relating to the three-dimensional or industrially produced designs one should instead make use of and refer to 'design rights' which deal specifically with the industrial application of design products.

Copyright advantages and disadvantages

As copyright comes into operation automatically when a simple drawing or work is created, cost and time-consuming registration formalities are avoided. Any copyright ownership should be clearly marked on the work to warn anybody viewing the work that it cannot be reproduced—in part or in full—without the permission of the original creator or copyright owners. As the copyright material is not officially registered, this is the only way of informing others that the work is protected by copyright. The marking of a copyright claim onto the work is also relevant to the issue of damages and proving secondary infringement.

At the same time it should be remembered that copyright does not stop others from arriving at the same original idea—independently—and also claiming copyright. It only gives the owner the right to stop someone else from copying or reproducing the work.

To prove the originality and copyright of a specific work, it is the responsibility of the creator to prove the details, e.g. the creation date, to a court. The general advice is to deposit a copy with a bank or solicitor or send a copy of the work to oneself by registered post—leaving the envelope unopened on its return and this will establish that the work existed at a specific time.[6]

Alternatively, it can often be more practical if a designer creates numerous designs each season, to set up an in-house design register whereby each design created is allocated a unique design number which is recorded on the design drawing itself together with the creator's name and date. A central design register should be created and kept up to date by someone of responsibility in the design department, listing designs created by date, design number, illustration and any relevant details. In cases of having to prove copyright ownership and creation date, the in-house design register will often prove a valuable tool. The in-house design register should however be established *in addition* to *original* design documents and drawings, which must not be replaced by copies.

Ideas and copyright

It should also be highlighted that although a work itself may be protected by copyright, the general rule is that the idea behind it is not. Furthermore, to benefit from copyright, something must be expressed in some tangible form or other, be it a simple drawing or a complete work.

For example, if a person makes a speech and presents the audience with his own theory for doubling Britain's clothing exports, although the speech may be original, he cannot prevent others from repeating his ideas (unless the speech is recorded in some way), even if he is not given credit for them. However, if he sets out the concept in writing and the written version is protected by copyright it cannot be copied without permission.

The application of copyright for the fashion industry

Design work within the clothing industry which will be protected by copyright is generally work such as original sketches and design drawings (regarded as design documents), textile design, surface decoration (e.g. knitwear patterns), two-dimensional dressmaking patterns, labels, transfers and trade advertisements but excludes sketches and drawings of non-artistic work, i.e. work which is not original.

If a company is only producing one or two items incorporating the design and these are intended to be unique—and the underlying design is an artistic work—the articles are generally regarded as works of artistic craftsmanship, i.e. not made by industrial process and the limited number of articles or garments will be protected under the copyright law.[10] If the design is instead produced on a larger scale using industrial processes, the original design drawing or document will maintain copyright protection, whilst garments or any three-dimensional articles are protected via the UK 'design right' legislation (see section 4.2).

Although copyright protection appears to have fairly limited applications for the clothing and textile industry, the following case of a British opera house versus a nationwide multiple retail/mail order company, illustrates some of the copyright implications for the fashion business.

The effect of international copyright conventions

As a result of the United Kingdom being a signatory to a number of international copyright conventions, British designers are entitled to copyright protection in other member states of certain international conventions such as the Berne Convention and the Universal Copyright Convention (UCC) (see section 1.6).

CASE STUDY

UK copyright case study

A well-established multiple retail and mail order company was, in December of 1993, served with High Court writs alleging infringement of copyright designs used in productions staged by a British opera house and ballet company.

A shirt selling at £36.99 by the retail organisation was alleged to be substantially copied from a section of artwork in costume designs used since 1990/91 in productions of 'The Nutcracker' in the UK. It was this artwork—based on original colour drawing designs—that the fashion retailer was accused of having copied onto clothing selling through its retail and mail order businesses.

The opera house concerned with the ballet production sought damages and the destruction of the garments which it alleged infringed the copyrights it owned.

Within four weeks of the writ being issued the opera house achieved 'substantial out of court settlement after the retail company admitted copying the designs used in the ballet production' and furthermore, the retail chain agreed to pay damages and withdraw the garments from sale once the stocks were used up, supposedly paying the opera house a royalty of all sales relating to the disputed artwork.

Reproduced with the permission of Drapers Record, © December 4 and 25, 1993

The general benefit for member countries under international agreements is that any copyright protection offered to a country's own nationals and businesses must also be given to copyright holders from other convention nations. In countries that provide automatic copyright legislation similar to that of the United Kingdom, British fashion businesses can claim statutory copyright on the basis of the international conventions.

However, it is wise to be aware that in some countries, e.g. the USA, the 'automatic copyright' structure does not exist in the same way as in the UK which in some instances can make the benefit of the international conventions an empty protection clause. The copyright structure of US law in many instances means that unless creators register their work they do not have sufficient enforcement rights. For example before an infringement suit may be filed in court, registration is necessary for works of US origin and for foreign works *not* originating in a Berne Union country (UK is a signatory to this Convention, refer to Box 1.1 for current members list). In effect, while registration is not a condition of protection timely registration establishes a public record of the work and may also provide a broader range of remedies in an infringement suit.

With regard to marking articles clearly with any copyright claim, it should also be noted that works published prior to March 1, 1989, *must* carry a notice of ownership with the international © symbol, year and ownership details or risk loss of copyright protection. For works published *after* the afore mentioned date the © marking is however optional, although it remains the responsibility of the copyright owner and does not require advance permission from the US Copyright Office.

The fairly simple US copyright registration/deposit system is outlined in the following case study.

CASE STUDY

US copyright registration for improved copyright enforcement

Unlike the UK, the USA has a formal copyright registration system which is generally simple and inexpensive. To register, a 'VA form' is filled in and sent together with required copies of the work to be protected, plus a registration fee of approximately US$20 (£13) to the US Copyright Office. To assist with completing the application form explanatory information circulars 40 and 40A are available directly from the Washington registry (or from some UK based legal offices—see Address List at the end of the book).

Copyright registration may be made at any time during the life of the US copyright, but can also be made even if no immediate publication is planned, e.g. in the interest of any future US business opportunities which should be protected against copying.

Note that unlike UK law, the successful side in a US lawsuit is not normally entitled to recover legal fees without prior written agreement of the other party. Such an agreement is often highly unlikely to be obtained from the accused infringer in a copyright case. Timely registration may also provide a broader range of remedies in an infringement dispute.

With US copyright registration a company or individual copyright owner is entitled to:

- *recover lawyer's fees (which can be up to US$100,000 or £65,000)*
- *recover profits lost as a result of the infringement or statutory damages.*

The US Copyright registration form (VA form) consists of only two A4 pages or nine sections with the following information fields:

1. *Title and nature of work.*
2. *Name of author(s), nationality/domicile, date of birth and author's contribution to the work.*
3. *Year of the work's completion and first publication (if applicable).*
4. *Copyright claimants.*
5. *Previous registration (if applicable).*
6. *Derivative work or compilation.*
7. *Payment details*
8. *Type of ownership/application certification.*
9. *Contact address for application and copyright certification.*

The completed VA form must be enclosed with the required number of works plus registration payment.

For fashion and textile products, US copyright protection applies mainly to artwork applied to clothing or any 'useful articles', fabric design, woven designs and lace designs.

Source: US Copyright Office, Washington

4.2 Design right

With the introduction of the new copyright law for the UK in 1988, the basic protection covering the vast majority of industrial designs has changed from copyright to design right. Note that design right is currently provided under UK legislation only and does not apply to any other countries.

This new protection category came into existence to give a new type of quasi-right to designs not protected by copyright under the CDPA 1988. It supports the protection of *original* design upon its creation—including any aspect relating to the design's shape or configuration (internal or external) of the whole *or* part of the article—whilst also protecting against unauthorised commercial copying of a design which is uncommon/original, be it the whole design or a substantial *part* of it.

The design right will automatically come into existence when a design is either recorded in a design document such as a sketch, or when a product is made to that design, e.g. a prototype garment. Like copyright, design right itself is not a monopoly right but the right to prevent copying. In reality, this could mean that for the same design, more than one creator may be able to claim design right provided both parties have arrived independently at the same original design.

The new design right differs from copyright by protecting the physical three-dimensional design and not *per se* the drawing from which it is created. Unlike copyright it is not a compulsory requirement for the original sketches or drawings to be produced in a court case, *unless* this was how the design right was first recorded.[3]

As design right does not protect surface decoration, textile designs do not qualify for design rights but remain to be protected by the original copyright protection and possibly registered design protection provided the designs qualify for registration.

Just as for copyright, when making use of design right it is important to make notes of when the design is first recorded in material form and when articles made to the design are first published (e.g. at a trade exhibition) or first made available for sale or hire. This information will be useful if someone attempts to challenge the existence or ownership of rights in the design, or should someone be found to infringe the design right, and the decision is made to take legal action.[7]

Exceptions to design right protection

The commercially oriented design right does not cover following types of work:

1. A method or principle of construction. These could be protected as know-how or possibly as patents (if they meet the statutory requirements).
2. Features of shape or configuration that relate to another article which 'must fit' and 'must match' that other article. This means a design where features of shape or configuration of a product are determined by another article, to which the product is to be connected or form an integral part.
3. Decoration on the surface of a product. For industrial designs with eye appeal these are instead covered by registered design and/or statutory copyright.[3]

Protection period of design right

In an attempt to strike an appropriate balance between the exclusive rights of a designer and the public interest in allowing healthy commercial competition, design right involves certain limitations in ways of time-scale.

The protection period is restricted to 10 years from the article's first marketing with an overall protection limit of 15 years from the date when the design was first recorded in a design document or an article was first made to the design.

After the first five years of marketing the industrial design, provision is made by the law for anyone during the *last* five years of the design right term to obtain a 'licence of right'. In general, this means that if during the design right period of 10 years from first marketing the product, the original design is infringed by the unauthorised copying and making of articles to the design—including the unauthorised trading in such articles—the design right owner has the right to take civil action in the courts, seeking damages, an injunction or other forms of compensation.[11]

Licence of right

The 'licence of right' provision comes into force after the first five years of marketing an industrial article for which design right is claimed. During the last five years of the protected 10-year marketing period anyone will be entitled, on application, to a licence to make and sell articles copying the design although the proprietor will not be obliged to make any design drawings or know-how available to the licensed copier.[7]

Should the owner of design rights at first be hesitant in granting a licence, e.g. by viewing it as a way of protecting his intellectual property, it should be considered that a licence can often be more advantageous than it would first appear. For example, if a licence is granted on a royalty basis to a competitor in a similar field, the competitor will first of all have to absorb the cost of royalties into the product which could be disadvantageous in terms of production costs and selling price. Secondly, while the licence does create competition for the original design right holder, it will also be earning the originator additional money through royalty payments.

In a case where the design right owner is unwilling to grant a 'licence of right' or the licence terms cannot be agreed, certain procedures are set out by the design right legislation whereby proper terms may be determined independently. In many cases this will typically be settled by the Comptroller General of Patents, Designs and Trade Marks, who will fix the royalty to be paid to the owner of the design right.

Infringing copies of design right garments

Keeping in mind that whilst design right gives the creator or design owner the *exclusive* right to reproduce the design for commercial purposes, based on copyright control of the design, the design right is *not* a right of monopoly. Therefore in exceptional cases, two or more parties may have a design right in the same design provided that each has created and arrived at the design independently and without any form or means of copying.

To establish that infringement of a garment design has occurred, it must be shown that there is substantial similarity between the original and the copy, or that the copy appears in the eye of a non-specialist to reproduce substantial parts of the original design.

When assessing whether or not one garment is a copy of another, UK legislation requires both an objective test of derivation and a subjective test of substantial similarity to be applied. Both are then combined to produce a valued judgement which will effectively establish whether on a balance of probabilities, the alleged infringing article was or was not produced by reference to and derived from the original.[3]

In general, the design right is considered to have been infringed by any person who without a licence agreement from the design right owner is making articles to the design or who makes a design document to enable others to reproduce the design. An infringement may be direct or indirect and include importing or proposing to import articles into the UK for commercial purposes, storing such infringing articles or any means of selling or hiring such articles.

Practical checklist for design right protection

The fact that design right is an automatic right, not officially registered, means that to claim intellectual ownership in a court of law, as with copyright protection, it is the responsibility of the originator to prove his or her rights.

To prove ownership of design in cases of infringement, it can be of ultimate importance that clothing companies, working with original industrial design, record their creations and sufficient details at the time of creation. A number of professional organisations specialising in intellectual property protection will often assist members in this area. And whilst any business guidelines for design information to be recorded may appear rather simple, these are the details which companies often fail to record properly thereby weakening their protection rights leaving the company unable to provide crucial proof in a design right dispute under current legislation.[3]

One intellectual property organisation specialising in assisting fashion companies is the Fashion Design Protection Association, who recommend the following protection checklist for original designs (note a similar checklist can be used for works protected by copyright):

1. All original sketches and drawings must be kept—not just a reference record or costing sheet drawings.
2. All sketches and drawings must be signed and dated by the designer at the time they are made.
3. Where the first embodiment of the design is in an actual garment this first garment must be kept in a safe place. A label should be securely attached to it signed and dated by the designer at the time the garment was made.
4. A record book of all the designs should be kept. This design register should record:
   (a) the design number—to identify the design;
   (b) the name of the designer;
   (c) the date the design was made;
   (d) the date when the first garment was produced;
   (e) the date that the design was first offered or sold;
   (f) the date of the first order and the order number—thereby fixing the date the first sale took place.
5. The design register should be properly bound and updated on a daily basis so that evidence of the sequential creation of designs is available. The task of maintaining the record book should be that of a responsible person within the company.
6. Proper written contracts of employment with designers should be maintained, making it clear who owns the designs created by the designer.
7. Written assignments must be recorded with respect to designs produced by independent designers or freelance organisations.
8. Designs made by the company directors who have no formal contracts of employment must be assigned to the company.

Reproduced with the permission of the Fashion Design Protection Association, London © FDPA, 1996

4.3 Summary of statutory protection rights

Statutory rights in the United Kingdom automatically arise by legislative provision when a work is created with no need for official recording. The two categories of unregistered protection rights available to designers and companies in the United Kingdom under the latest 1988 legislation are copyright and design right.

Copyright comes into operation automatically when an original drawing or work is created (including computer-generated works). It applies to artistic works which include works by artistic craftsmanship.

The advantage of copyright arising automatically is that it does not involve any time or cost-consuming formal registration procedures.

The purpose of copyright claim is to prevent the reproduction of a work be it completely, in part or adapted form without the permission of

CASE STUDY

Design right: Retail group and the womens wear coat design

In September 1991, a court instructed a retail store group to remove a range of women's raincoats from all 82 of its stores, whilst a claim of design right infringement from a well-known coat design company was being resolved.

The coat manufacturer claimed that the store group had stopped ordering its design, part of the firm's up-market branded range, only to start stocking an alleged replica at a cheaper price a few months later, which featured the vast majority of the distinctive design elements from the original raincoat design. The manufacturer's counsel presented to the court the argument that if the 'copied' version of the coat remained in the retailer's stores at the cheaper price point, other independent outlets supplied with the same raincoat design might demand that the prices of their branded coats be dropped too, which would harm the manufacturer's reputation.

In addition the coat company had recently invested in a £50,000 national advertising campaign and had issued a catalogue to its 270 customers highlighting their coat design now involved in the infringement dispute. Therefore if the retail store group continued to stock the coat it would be benefiting from the wide-scale campaign launched by the rain wear company.

Although the retailer's counsel said that removing the alleged copies would 'not be simple' and would result in lost sales for the retail group, the injunction was granted for all coats to be removed from the department store chain.

In this design right case no further court hearings were reported and it appears that, as in the majority of design and copyright disputes, the companies involved reached a mutual agreement satisfactory to both parties in solving the alleged design right infringement.

Reproduced with the permission of Drapers Record, © September 28, 1991

CASE STUDY

Design right: Infringement: part of the original design produced

The following case study illustrates how design right protection can be applied to 'substantially similar' designs, when from a viewpoint of garment construction and assembly an article is not **technically** *a copy. But viewed* **aesthetically** *the garment may appear in the eyes of a non-specialist, e.g. the consumer, to be of the same design.*

This case is also an example of how the clothing industry often settles copyright issues, by reaching an agreement out of court to avoid adverse publicity, independent of whether the alleged infringer copied deliberately or was actually unaware of the original design's existence.

Part of the original design reproduced (1992)

Following the claim by a design company that part of a garment design had been reproduced by merchandise sold by a major retail chain, the garment was withdrawn from all retail outlets. The garment, a body, was spotted by the designer of a clothing design company, who claimed that the body's distinctive lattice front was the same as one designed for a previous collection, still being produced by her company.

Using the design right provisions under the CDPA 1988, the design company maintained that though structurally the panels of its body were substantially different from garments sold by the multiple retailer, part of its original design had been reproduced. The retailer did not contest the design issue and withdrew the offending garment as a gesture of goodwill without any admission that deliberate copying had occurred.

Reproduced by permission of Drapers Record, © April 11, 1992

the creator/owner. Alternatively, the copyright holder may seek financial remedy for any such reproductions.

Copyright will last for the lifetime of the creator plus 70 years thereafter. In the case of infringement it is the responsibility of the creator to prove the ownership and existence of copyright and that the work has been copied. For that purpose when working with original design it is strongly recommended that simple in-house design records are maintained to prove ownership and date of creation.

More than one copyright can exist for the highly similar work, if each creator has arrived at the work independently. While copyright does *not* cover works where the underlying design is non-artistic, three-dimensional *artistic* works where copyright does apply include sculptures, models and works of artistic craftsmanship.

Where copyright protected work is reproduced in larger quantities or by industrial processes, articles are regarded as 'industrial design'. And although copyright may protect the *drawing* of an industrial design of artistic merit, it does not generally protect the industrial article. In case of industrially produced designs one should instead make use of 'design rights' which deal specifically with the industrial application of design products.

Fields in the fashion industry where copyright ownership is applicable include: two-dimensional design work such as original sketches (except sketches of the shape of a garment of little or no aesthetic quality), fashion illustrations, textile design, surface design, dressmaking patterns, labels, transfers and trade advertisements and also garments produced only once or twice as unique items of craftsmanship.

Design right is a new protection type introduced with the 1988 Act to offer protection for original, industrial design articles. Protection is given to the shape or configuration (whether internal or external) of the whole *or part* of the designed article.

Design right protection is concerned with original industrial design, focusing on the actual article with no mandatory requirement for original drawings to be produced to claim ownership, *unless* that was how the design was first recorded. Alternatively, three-dimensional articles such as prototype or production garments of the design can be used to prove design right, together with material proving first marketing/publication date, promotional adverts and PR catalogues.

Design right protection lasts for up to 10 years from the first marketing or 15 years if not made available commercially with the exclusive rights to reproduce the design, subject to any 'licence of right' provisions during the last five years of the 10-year protection period from first marketing date. 'Licence of right' can be obtained by other companies who are obliged to pay royalties for the licence.

Whilst design right for industrial design is copyright-based and not a monopoly for original industrial design, design right is a particularly British protection type not found in other countries, and as such is not supported by any international copyright conventions.

In individual European countries the gap in protection of industrial design is, in some instances, covered by various short-term protection categories, as for example 'petty patents' or 'utility models' with some formal registration systems rather than automatic protection rights. However, recent legislative developments within the European Union will in the near future facilitate protection of original industrial designs via Community design protection, valid throughout all EU Member States (see Chapter 7).

5

REGISTERED PROTECTION RIGHTS

The legislation available for the categories of registered protection rights are concerned with protection of intellectual property applied commercially or industrially.

The three categories of registered protection available in the United Kingdom are:

1. **Patents** – concerned with technical inventions.
2. **Registered design** – the protection of aesthetic elements in original industrial design emphasising appearance, including features of shape and patterns.
3. **Registered trade marks** – for logo and/or brand names.

When considering whether to make use of patents or registered design, extreme care must be taken to avoid premature publication or 'premature disclosure' (described in Chapter 3), which can result in the registration application being declared invalid. This is simply because one of the crucial elements for granting the registration, is the requirement that the work must be 'new' and *un*published prior to filing the application.

Other general aspects should also be considered when using registration facilities for intellectual property. Registered work, in cases of dispute, benefit from a much stronger legal standpoint and have the official registration to prove ownership compared to an unregistered design right. However, the formal registration system also involves certain time and cost factors which should qualify and relate to the commercial needs of the organisation in its own business context. In other words, registration should not be a goal in itself—the intellectual property owner should be quite clear about the purpose and benefits of the registration as a business asset.

Furthermore, having obtained registration of a patent, design or trade mark does not mean that the official registry in some way will 'police' the rights of proprietors. Instead, legislation provides the framework and facilities which allow designers, inventors and businesses to ensure their interests can be protected—at the responsibility of the registration owner(s).

5.1 Patents

Under the UK patent system, this is a monopoly right to an invention and can be granted through renewal up to a maximum of 20 years. To qualify for a patent the invention must be concerned with the composition, construction or manufacture of a substance, article, apparatus or with an industrial type of process—all types being distinct from artistic creations, mathematical methods, business schemes or other purely mental acts.[8]

Patented inventions are often associated with major scientific advances or technical gadgets. However, in many instances this view is oversimplified as virtually any kind of machine, product and process—across the industrial spectrum—can be patented provided it satisfies the following criteria.

It must be new, inventive, capable of industrial application and not be part of any excluded concept categories.[12]

It must be *new*, meaning not previously published. The invention's novelty relates not only to the UK territory in order to qualify for a UK patent. According to the 1977 Patent Act specification of the term 'new' is understood as 'the state of the art . . . whether in the United Kingdom *or elsewhere*'.

It must be *inventive*: of a non-obvious character which involves an inventive step, compared to the state of the art—all concepts already known.

It must be capable of *industrial application* and in this instance 'industrial' must be interpreted in its broadest sense. The invention must involve the practical form of an apparatus, product or device.

It must not belong to *'excluded' patent categories* means that an invention which is simply a discovery or a scientific theory, a method of doing business or a computer program will not be patentable. However, if the *abstract concept* involves the physical outward features of a product or device—*provided* they are not merely aesthetic features—it may be possible to obtain a patent. Any *aesthetic appearance* of an article would instead be suitable for design registration.

Registration procedure

It is important to highlight that in the case of patent applications, due to the legal complexities involved in submitting legally correct and complete patent applications, inexperienced individuals should not attempt to file application. It must be stressed that patent application should be entrusted to a professional patent agent with the necessary expertise and legal knowledge.

However, for the benefit of understanding the general processes involved in filing a patent application in the UK, the following main procedures have been outlined:

- filing the application;
- preliminary search and publication;
- substantive examination;
- patent notification;
- publication.[12]

Filing the application

Under the existing patent law applications have to be made in a particular way using official forms as supplied by the patent office; they consist of:

1. the patent request;
2. identification details of the applicant;
3. clear and complete description of the invention;
4. filing fee.

The description and wording of the invention are extremely important and must essentially be legally 'watertight'—see example on page 56. To cover all possible complexities of the law a patent agent should always be used to draw up the patent application and prosecute it.

Once the complete application is filed with the Patent Office a 'filing date' is issued or if the application is based on a previous UK or overseas application filed up to 12 months earlier, then the earlier date will be used as official 'priority date'.

During the 12 months following the application filing or priority date the inventor/owner can explore the commercial value of the invention, seek financing or further development without the risk of

EXAMPLE

The importance of wording a patent claim

If the claims in a patent application are not carefully worded they may allow a rival to copy an idea. For example a tool had been patented whereby removing the rear wheels and remounting them in parallel with the front wheels led to the creation of another type of tool ultimately providing the user with a two-in-one solution. A similar concept later appeared from a competitor, on which the front wheels could be remounted in parallel with the rear wheels. The patent proprietors took the inventor of the rival tool to court alleging an infringement of their patent. Decision: The court decided that the rival had clearly taken the idea but the company holding the official registration had patented only the idea of changing round the back wheels, not the front, so there was no infringement of the patent.

EXAMPLE

Initial patent application for a clothing product: the skirt/bag by Ici La Fille (priority application: GB 9106294.3)

The patent application has been filed for a wrap-around leather skirt design which converts into a shoulder bag. The item has been copyrighted and a patent application filed to prevent copies. Wholesale price of the original version is approximately £45, while a less expensive version in nylon/Lycra will make the style more accessible to the high street by wholesaling for £20–30.[12]

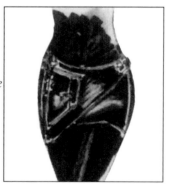

Reproduced with the permission of Drapers Record, © May 4, 1991

---

losing any ownership rights from showing the invention publicly—see example above. If the invention proprietor(s) within the one-year period decide to progress with the patent application a search fee is paid and the invention progresses to the next level of the registration process.

Preliminary search and early publication

Based on the invention specification supplied, the Patent Office will carry out a formal and technical preliminary examination plus a search to ensure the invention is indeed new and does not interfere with existing patents. In instances of opposition a Search Report is issued which allows the applicant to file any description amendments and claims.

Next, the application is published in print—within 18 months of the filing date—to allow public access to invention claims and the opportunity to contest the patent application.

Substantive examination

Within six months of the early publication, the Patent Office must carry out the final stage before the patent is granted. The invention will be checked in detail to ensure it meets all relevant legal requirements according to the CDPA 1988. Prior to this stage, an examination fee must be paid to the Patent Office.

Patent notification

Provided all of the above stages are satisfied the patent is granted, the specification republished and official monopoly claims accepted. The initial patent is valid for a period of four years from the priority date, thereafter renewal is possible up to a maximum of 20 years from the application date.

Publication

The specification in its final form together with other necessary details are held at the Patent Office Library and other UK libraries.

During the various stages of patent processing the applicant has options for amending or clarifying specification claims if necessary. After the patent is granted any person may still challenge the monopoly claims by applying to the appropriate comptroller or the courts. The following example, taken from the fibre technology sector, illustrates a patent dispute where monopoly rights are opposed. In this instance the patent ownership was challenged not only on a national but a European level (see Chapter 7 for European intellectual property developments and existing legislation structures).

CASE STUDY

Fibre technology dispute

TENCEL®

Tencel is one of the new high-tech fashion fibres of the 1990s. The branded lyocell fibre is particularly attractive due to its strength, absorbency, lightweight and easy-care properties of being machine washable, whilst having a distinctly soft feel.

But during the early years of Courtaulds Fibre launching the Tencel fibre it has also been at the centre of a patent dispute between producers Courtaulds in the UK and Lenzing based in Austria. The patent dispute, first reported in the trade press in July 1994, focused on part of the technology involved in production of the lyocell fibre.

By late 1994, the initial patent challenge from the British company was rejected by the European Patents Office (EPO) and Lenzing maintained the technological monopoly rights.

However, following the process of appeal the dispute ended in 1996, with the EPO reversing the earlier decision of sole rights for the Austrian company as being invalid. The board of appeal instead awarded shared rights. The new ruling meant that Courtaulds could continue to produce their branded Tencel fibre as well as Lenzing producing lyocell fibres using the same technological process.

Reproduced with the permission of Tencel Fibres Europe, © 1994

Cost of a patent registration

When issuing the official application forms the Patent Office will also be able to confirm current up-to-date fees which are subject to yearly adjustments. But an approximate indication of the fees related to obtaining a patent in the United Kingdom are as follows. The initial filing fee for an application is approximately £25 with the initial search and the substantive examination stages approximately £130 each. When the patent is granted annual renewal fees are paid on a sliding scale. For example the fifth year of the patent would be around £150 and the 20th and last year £450. To keep a patent in force over a 20-year period the total fees would typically come to around £4,000.

Patent proprietors can of course discontinue a patent at any stage by not paying the renewal fees, alternatively a patent which has lapsed through non-payment may be reinstated within a certain period of time.

Time factors

The time before a patent is granted varies between applications but as a rough guide the preliminary Search Report will be issued within three months after request. Early publication will be within 18 months after filing an application and substantive examination about 18 months after publication. The granting of patents follow after any official objections are met and rectified, such as minor changes in wording or patent claims.

All stages between the filing date up to the granting of a patent must be completed within four-and-a-half years of the first filing date. However, substantially faster granting of patents is possible provided the applicant can state a case for accelerated processing.

Advantages and disadvantages of patents

Before deciding to apply for a patent it should be clear to the applicant that the ultimate aim of inventions is not to achieve patents, and that a patent does by no means guarantee levels of financial benefit. The creator can also choose other forms of protection, by keeping the invention secret whilst in the meantime developing and exploiting the concept further. But of course once the product of a non-patented invention is placed in the market-place it is there for everyone to see and can be imitated (subject to statutory copyright or design right claims).

The strength of a patent relates to the monopoly of rights and commercial exploitation which, through patent renewal, may last for up to 20 years, giving the opportunity to patent holders to negotiate long-term licence agreements and also the protection against individuals or companies who at a later date, by completely independent means, develop and try to claim invention rights for the same invention as the original patent holder. In such instances the patent owner has the right to enforce his monopoly of protection by use of the patent. The Patent Office itself is also likely to reject the later application based on its searches, due to not meeting the criteria that it 'must be new and inventive'.

On reflection, it is therefore important for inventors always to be up to date and aware of both *new* and *existing patents* and *recent developments*, not to waste time and resources on inventions already patented or risk being sued for infringement.

An international advantage of the UK patent system is via international patent conventions. Should a UK patent holder wish to file an overseas application within 12 months of the British application date, he or she can state the earlier UK filing date as 'priority date' which will affect others who may have invented the same concept in the interim period and may be trying to claim their own monopoly rights.

Compared to other categories of intellectual property, international patent legislation is at an advanced stage of development. Already for some years it has been possible to apply for European (EPC) and world-wide patents (PCT) by filing one application only. Already over 90% of the world's patent applications and patents are administered by the European Patent Office, the Japanese Patent Office and the United States Patent and Trade Mark Office.

Due to the larger scale of invention, search and examination involved in international patents, cost levels are also considerably higher. In comparison the cost of achieving a European patent is approximately 10 times higher than a national UK patent, plus the additional cost of £150–200 per designation country.

Although the patent cost is considerably higher on a European scale it should be viewed from the perspective that on the basis of *one* application—only one patent agent's fee—and one examining procedure, a patent can be achieved in up to 17 countries, namely Austria, Belgium, Denmark, France, Germany, Greece, Ireland, Italy, Liechtenstein, Luxembourg, Monaco, Netherlands, Portugal, Spain, Sweden, Switzerland and the United Kingdom.

The clothing industry and patent protection

The majority of industrially produced clothing is the result of creative innovation rather than invention, thereby more applicable protection types for the fashion industry are found with design right and registered design rights.

Should a fashion company invent a garment which qualifies for patent protection, although protection rights commence from the date of patent

EXAMPLE

Patents for clothing products

Patent example: 'self-supporting stockings' by H Flude & Co (Hinckley) and J.C. Humphreys. Priority application 9000212, date: January 5, 1990 (Patent: GB 2258135): 'The invention refers to a method of producing a self-supporting stocking, where the stocking is supported by the interior of a welt ring facing radially outward from the stocking and rotated about its longitudinal axis while a silicone material is applied to the welt so as to form a stripe'.

Reproduced with the permission of H Flude & Co (Hinckley) Ltd

Patent pending for design technique of 'The Stowaway Range' by Rosemary Moore (Patent ref.: 9606942.2): Stowaway® is the registered trade mark for a resort wear

range of clothes which neatly fold into their own fist-sized integral pocket. The idea is to allow the stowed garment packets to be threaded onto a belt and carried anywhere—perfect for travelling light.

The concept created by Rosemary Moore, was launched for spring/ summer 1997 and combines fashion design and packaging into lightweight garments ideal for travelling and including a collection in stretch jersey fabric with swimwear, gym and resort wear such as dresses, leggings, shorts, bikinis, swimsuits and T-shirts. Garments are made in two textiles: a reversible stretch Lycra jersey and a single dyed stretch Tactel/Lycra mix which, in combination with body heat, allows the creases to fall out within seconds of wearing the garment.

The Stowaway range includes Stowaway Resort, Street and Active ranges— from bright beach wear to glamorous evening wear.

Reproduced with the permission of Rosemary Moore, Stowaway Ltd

The Stowaway® range—combining design and packaging concept
(Patent pending: 9606942.2):

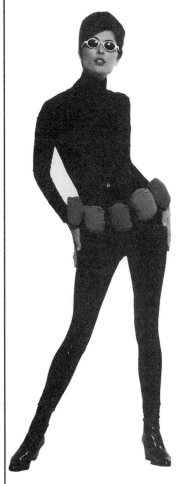 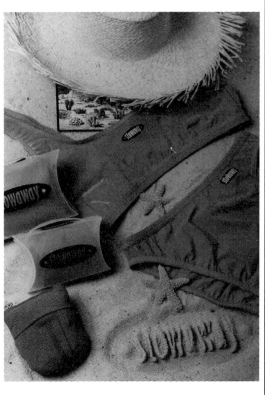

Reproduced with the permission of Rosemary Moore, Stowaway Ltd

application, a major factor to consider is the comparatively long time it takes for achieving the patent. The commercial product strategy should therefore be long-term rather than short-lived commercial use, as the latter may not recoup patent costs sufficiently in a short time span.

The example on page 61 shows however that patents *can* be applied to less revolutionary inventions such as industrial clothing products.

5.2 Registered design

While patents protect the core of a product or process, the outward shape or decorative appearance of products can, in the United Kingdom, be protected either by registered design or (unregistered) design right. Whereas the automatic protection rights rely on the owners to prove their ownership right in the event of IP disputes, officially registered designs stand legally much stronger and clearer in holding ownership rights. The protection which can be achieved through design registration is in *addition* to the protection against copying under design right. Although it is important to remember that design right does not protect textile surface decoration, in which case registered design protection should be used to protect original surface designs.

A successful design registration will grant protection for an initial period of five years and may be extended in four five-year terms up to a maximum of 25 years. In comparison, automatic design right only offers exclusive rights during the first 10 years of marketing. Over the last five years of the maximum 10-year protection, the design right owner is legally obliged, on application, to issue licences of right to others wishing to reproduce and market the design.

Registered design protection is available for new, aesthetic and original standalone designs. The features which can be protected by registration are the design elements of 'shape', 'configuration', 'pattern' or 'ornament' which compared to existing or earlier designs of the same article type 'must make a materially different appeal to the eye when each article is viewed as a whole'.[5]

The essential criteria—as for all types of registered intellectual property—remains the specification of the concept being 'new' at the date of filing application. It must not previously have been published, offered for sale or sold in the UK, which is why any unauthorised premature disclosure of the design can bar an application for registered design, a simple point but crucial to remember as once the design is published or disclosed it will be too late to try and obtain the registration.

Once the design registration is granted the IP proprietor(s) obtain the exclusive right to make, import, sell or hire out any article to which the design has been applied or to let others use the design under terms agreed with the registered owner.

Some groups of design work which are excluded from design registration are specified for works which are purely functional and lack the element of creativity and aesthetic appearance. Purely functional designs *or* variations commonly used in the industry belong to excluded registration categories. This is due to the lack of 'novelty' which generally involves more skill, labour and original thought than the routine manipulation of well-established design elements.

Registered 'set' of designs

Occasionally a certain design may be applied to two or more articles as a 'set'. To classify as such the set must (a) be sold, or intended for use, together and (b) share a 'common identity' of design. If the individual articles of a set are linked by very similar surface decoration, but consist of different shapes, protection can be claimed solely for the 'pattern or ornament' of the design set but not for the 'shape and configuration'. The level of design protection applied to the registration of a 'set' is the same as would have been gained from registering the design for each article individually.[10]

Procedure for registered design applications

The official application form 'Designs Form 2A' is issued by the Patent Office together with general application guidelines, statement of novelty specification and the list of fees related to processing the registration. Far from presenting numerous pages to be completed, the application form itself is merely two A4 pages, with a clear layout and written in language easy to understand. The 10 information sections to be completed involve the following:

1. design reference;
2. full name and address of applicant(s);
3. corporation status (if applicable);
4. name of agent (if applicable);
5. design applied to article type (single vs. set of articles);
6. name concisely the article design is being applied to;
7. state previous registration of identical design to another article, if applicable;
8. previous design's registration number (for modifications/variations);
9. priority date from previous application made in a design convention country (within the last six months);
10. details of person filing overseas application (if made by someone other than the applicant for the UK design registration).

Finally, the preprinted declaration of ownership must be signed and dated.

Source: The Patent Office/Design Registry, UK

To file an application the official form is accompanied by four identical specimens or representations of the design to be registered plus a statement of the design's novelty (not applicable for textiles or lace) and the prescribed fee to process the application. The 'statement of novelty' is formally specified to ensure all applications follow a certain description structure and format.

Once the application is filed with the Designs Registry, the processing system follows certain stages before the UK registration is granted.

Submission of the application

Prior to publication of the work the designer or owner(s) of the design must file the application with the Design Registry in London and must include the design representation or specimens, the registration fee and a statement of the design for which novelty is claimed.

An official receipt is issued and sent to the applicant, with the details of filing date and number. The receipt details are *not* a Certificate of Registration but are important if wishing to claim 'priority' date for other applications being made overseas for the same design concept. The receipt number identifies the application in the Registry's records and until the official registration is granted can be used for marking articles (i.e. 'pending Design Registration no. 12345').

It is important to remember that it is an offence to mark articles as registered if they are not, or if a registration has lapsed or expired. The article marking must therefore clearly state the application status by use of

The novelty statement required for your application should be expressed in terms of shape, configuration, pattern or ornament and may relate to the article as a whole, or a particular part of the article. These are the only features which may be protected by the registration of the design and any statement relating to a method of constructing the article or to advantages in its use is inadmissible. A description of the article is not required and should not be included with the novelty statement. Two alternative forms of wording set out below suitably express the design features which may be claimed as novel and may be found helpful in completing the statement of novelty.

Examples of Statements of Novelty:

example 1:   The feature(s) of the design for which novelty is claimed is/are the ★ [shape, configuration, pattern and ornament] applied to the article as shown in the representation.

★*Omit any of these features not present in the design or not being claimed.*

example 2:   The feature(s) of the design for which novelty is claimed is/are the ★ [shape, configuration, pattern and ornament] of the part(s) of the article as shown [coloured blue/ringed in red] in the representation.

★ *Clearly identify the part(s) on all views. Apply either a light blue permanent wash carefully and evenly to the part(s) or ring in red if that will precisely identify the part(s).*

The statement can now be made on a separate sheet of paper although it must be incorporated onto the representations prior to registration. The statement must not be embodied in a letter relating to other matters.

Source: The Patent Office ('Statement of Novelty')

the description 'pending' together with the type of ownership claim, in this case 'design registration'.

Examination and search

To establish that the design is 'new' a formal examination and aesthetically-based search is carried out among existing design registrations, published periodicals, catalogues, etc. Although the search spans widely, it cannot be exhaustive or guarantee that no one will challenge the registration.

If the design is found not to be 'new' or certain documentary amendments are necessary to bring the application in line with standards, notification is forwarded to the applicant. Once all the documents are in order the registration can officially be granted.

Note that selected categories of design are granted registration *without a search*. These include checks and stripe patterns applied to 'textile articles' as well as lace designs - see following example:

EXAMPLE

Design registration: goods classified as 'textile articles' relating to fashion and textile industries

For the purpose of design registration of goods which classify as 'textile articles' and for which protection required may be limited to features of pattern and ornament:

- *textile piece goods*
- *knitted piece goods (other than lace)*
- *plastic piece goods (woven, netted or printed)*
- *shawls, handkerchiefs and elastic web*
- *textile squares to be made up into articles.*

The following articles, if made of textile material or from plastics piece goods (woven, netted or printed): ribbons, saries, sarongs, trimmings.[5]

Certificate of Registration

If no objections follow the formal search, a Certificate of Registration will be issued, initially valid for five years. The ownership belongs to the person or organisation to whom the Certificate of Registration is issued (based on information stated on the original application form).

Renewals

It is the responsibility of the design proprietor to renew registered designs by forwarding the necessary fees accompanied with specific renewal forms three months before the current registration expires. In cases where registration has lapsed through non-payment, the registration rights may be re-established within certain time limits, provided the Registrar is 'satisfied that reasonable care was taken by the design proprietor to maintain the protection'.[5]

Assignments and licences

Arrangements concerning the registered design, such as assignment, licence, mortgage or other matters affecting the rights, must be filed with the Designs Registry.[10] If such changes are *not* recorded with the Registry, in the instance of infringement disputes, the person relying on the licence transaction as a basis for his/her entitlement to bring the legal action may not be entitled to do so.

Time factors

Design registration usually takes about four months from the filing date with a maximum time allowed of 12 months for the proprietor(s) to bring in order an application, e.g. in relation to objections. Applications not in order within 15 months of the filing date will have to be abandoned and cannot then be registered.

Once the design registration is granted, protection is valid for five years from the date of filing. Registration renewal is available for five-year periods up to a maximum of 25 years.

Registration costs

The initial application costs range from £35–90 depending on the article category. Subject to annual adjustment the following amounts indicate a rough guideline for the cost elements related to registered designs:

1. single article not requiring a formal search (mainly lace, stripe or check articles) £35;
2. other single articles involving formal search procedure £60;
3. sets of articles £90.

The approximate renewal fee for the second five-year protection period is currently £130 and for a third period £210, increasing to £310 for the fourth period and for the fifth and final five-year term the fee is £450. Other fees relating to applications such as extension and correction of errors range between £20 to £50 apart from the restoration of a registered design (£120).

The additional costs involved when applying for registration, be it for a patent, design or trade mark, will often arise from the preparation of documents, article specimens and any legal fees towards patent agents and lawyers responsible for preparing the more central legal matters of an application, thereby assisting in making the ownership claims as 'water-tight' as possible against competition and possible interpretations.

Priority dates

Compared to the worldwide registration system available for patent registration, no 'world registration' system exists for industrial designs as yet. Instead, companies and individuals working with original designs may make use of Commonwealth legislation and international conventions which include larger groups of countries. These allow proprietors to claim 'priority' of registration from applications filed in other convention signatory states, provided the claim is made within six months after the earliest application.

An application which claims this 'priority' cannot then be invalidated on the basis of not being 'new', even if the design by now has been published or industrially applied in the UK, or if, in the same period, a competitor has produced a similar product.

Should the British register for any reason declare a priority claim invalid, be aware that for the UK application to progress, written assurance will be required from the applicant that the design has not been unduly published, manufactured or sold in the UK *prior* to filing the UK application. The claim of a registration priority date will mainly apply to proprietors not resident in the UK.

In connection with claims of priority date, UK residents should note that it is forbidden to file design applications abroad unless:

1. an application has been filed—for the same design—with the UK register not less than six weeks previously;
2. no directions have been given by the UK Registrar to prohibit or restrict the publication of the design (if so such directions must be revoked before filing the design application abroad);
3. the design owner has obtained a written permit from the UK Registrar to make an application outside the UK for that particular design.[5]

Countries which have implemented local legislation that allows UK design registrations to benefit from the same protection as granted to their own registered concepts are found mainly within the Commonwealth.

This avoids several national registration procedures, although some states require the completion of local formalities.

Under the International Convention for Protection of Industrial Property a wider range of countries exist, whereby the UK application may state 'priority' of registration for the same design filed at the earlier date in a 'Convention country'. The priority claim must be made within six months after the earliest application. (Note: the list of countries may change at any time and enquiries should be made to the enquiries desk of the Design Registry).

Registered design—advantages and disadvantages

In practice, the cost and time formalities involved with registering designs may discourage fashion and textile industries making use of this protection type, if working to comparatively short lead times and product life cycles, although the criteria of newness and non-publication prior to filing the application, do *not* restrict the company in marketing the design on the day following the filing of the application and before the official Certificate of Registration is granted.

When the design application is being processed—typically within a four-month period—articles can be manufactured, published and sold with no limitations and the ownership claim of the intellectual property can be noted by marking articles 'pending design registration'.

It may be argued that one disadvantage of registered design protection is that companies have to make the decision of whether or not to invest in registering the original design concept, without having first tested the sales appeal in the market-place. This argument may, however, be viewed in a similar manner as any sales projection and marketing assessment, where financial funds are committed before knowledge of the investment return and success rate. Also, the intellectual property owner may try to assess the level and long-term appeal of the design concept by discussing and receiving feedback from existing distributors or market development managers, provided that all parties involved clearly understand that the design is confidential and classified as company know-how.

The design registration itself does not diminish the basic protection provided through the statutory copyright and design right legislation. But one major advantage of using design registration in infringement disputes is that the proprietor does not need to prove copying has been carried out by the alleged infringer.

Box 5.1

Countries extending their protection to United Kingdom registered designs

(a)   Without the necessity of local registration

Anguila, Antigua, Belize, Bermuda, Botswana, British Indian Ocean Territory, British Virgin Islands, Brunei (awaiting confirmation), Cyprus, Dominica, Falklands Islands, Fiji, Gambia, Ghana, Gibraltar, Grenada, Guyana, Hong Kong, Kenya, Kiribati, Malaysia (including Sabah and Sarawak), St Christopher (St Kitts) Nevis, St Helena, St Lucia, St Vincent, Sierra Leone, Singapore, Solomon Islands, Swaziland, Tuvalu, Uganda, Vanuatu and Yemenite Arab Republic.

(b)   Countries requiring local reregistration of UK design

Guernsey (any time during UK registration), Jersey (within three years of registration in the UK), Malta (within four months of filing the UK application), Montserrat (any time during UK registration), Tanzania, Trinidad and Tobago (within three years of registration in the UK).

Note: The following countries have no provision in local law for design protection which may apply to UK design, either by local registration or reregistration: Cayman Islands, Mauritius and the Seychelles.

The extension of protection related to the above countries may change or terminate at any time after publication, confirm with the Design Registry.

Source: The Patent Office/Design Registry, UK

To prove infringement of a registered design it is sufficient to show that the infringer of the design rights has 'made articles to that design'. Even if the infringer arrived at that design independently and/or accidentally, he can still be restrained from using an industrial design that already exists. So in that sense, the first design originator does not have to prove any intentional copying or clearly similar 'interpretations' of the design. In comparison, cases argued on the basis of copyright do not provide the same possibility of restraint. If the copyright infringer arrives at the same design by a completely independent path and can prove this, he does not infringe the original owner's copyright.[13]

Another advantage of registered design legislation is the longer term protection available—up to 25 years—compared to only 10 years' protection under the automatic UK design right or 15 years from design creation. Of that 10-year time span only the *first* five years of publication

EXAMPLE

'The Multi-Body' by Gina Holt
Registration: 2053131
(priority date: January 4, 1996)

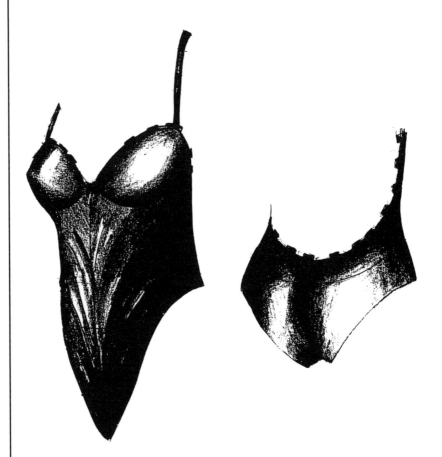

The novelty of the design consists of the numerous small loops incorporated into the 'multi-body' design both on the front and back of the garment whereby the shoulder straps can be repositioned and adapted to suit various necklines, e.g. backless evening dresses which would usually require strapless bra/lingerie to be worn.

Reproduced with the permission of Gina Elizabeth Holt BA (Hons), PGCE

Box 5.2

'Convention countries' for UK design registration purposes
(112 states as of September 1996)

Algeria	Egypt	Luxembourg	Slovenia
Argentina	Finland	Madagascar	South Africa
Australia	France	Malawi	Spain
Austria	Gabon	Malaysia	Sri Lanka
Bahamas	Gambia	Mali	Sudan
Bangladesh	Germany	Malta	Surinam
Barbados	Ghana	Mauritania	Sweden
Belarus	Greece	Mauritius	Switzerland
Belgium	Guinea	Mexico	Syria
Benin	Guinea-Bissau	Monaco	Tanzania
Brazil	Haiti	Mongolia,	Togo
Bulgaria	Hong Kong	People's	Trinidad and
Burkina Faso	Hungary	Rep. of	Tobago
Burundi	Iceland	Morocco	Tunisia
Cameroon	India	Netherlands	Turkey
Canada	Indonesia	New Zealand	Uganda
Central African	Iran	Niger	Ukraine
Republic	Iraq	Nigeria	Uruguay
Chad	Ireland	Norway	USA
Chile	Israel	Pakistan	Vatican
China, People's	Italy	Philippines	(Holy See)
Rep. of	Ivory Coast	Poland	Vietnam
Congo	Japan	Portugal	Yugoslavia
Croatia	Jordan	Romania	Zaire
Cuba	Kazakhstan	Russian	Zambia
Cyprus	Kenya	Federation	Zimbabwe
Czech	Korea (South)	Rwanda	
Republic	Lebanon	San Marino	Source: The
Czechoslovakia	Lesotho	Senegal	Patent Office/
Denmark	Libya	Singapore	Design Registry,
Dominican Rep.	Liechtenstein	Slovak Republic	UK

---

and marketing provide wholly exclusive rights for commercial exploitation to make, import, sell, hire and license the registered design(s). For the last five-year period of the automatic design right, intellectual property owner(s) are legally bound and *must* accommodate any requests under the 'licence of right' allowing other parties to produce and sell the design on a royalty basis.

The proprietor of a registered design is not subject to any 'licence of right' clause to the same extent as for a statutory design right, although any person may apply to the registry for a 'compulsory licence' in respect of a registered design. Such licence applications according to the CDPA 1988 may only be made provided 'that the design is *not* applied in the United Kingdom by any industrial process or means to the article in respect of which it is registered to such an extent as is reasonable in the circumstances of the case'.

By making use of the rights available under registered design legislation, proprietors have the opportunity of negotiating more long-term licence/royalty agreements within the 25-year term of registration. The benefit of licence agreements—especially for small size companies of limited financial means who produce highly original designs with international appeal—is that via the licence/royalty contracts design(s) can reach overseas markets and achieve very successful sales without the design company having to invest heavily in the area of production and overseas marketing. Instead a licence contract may in fact greatly assist small design companies to reap much wider financial benefits from their creative and original designs.

A further reason why fashion companies should consider registered design protection concerns industrially produced goods. The original drawings for a design to be used on textiles are protected under automatic copyright law as artistic works. However, when these designs are used on or incorporated in industrially produced textiles and fabrics for much larger quantities, the copyright criteria is usually exceeded and the automatic copyright protection does not apply in such cases. Compared with registered design and UK design right, the latter protection is also limited with regard to time (up to 15 years from creation *or* 10 years from first marketing)—design ownership is generally easier to prove through the use of registered design as well as by providing a longer term of exclusive rights for producing the design. Registration initially gives five years' monopoly but is renewable to a maximum of 25 years.[2]

5.3 Registered trade marks

It can be argued that using a trade mark to distinguish a company's goods does not itself give protection for the design of a product *per se*. However, by using a trade mark, designs can be linked closely with the firm and its reputation, as recognised by the latest Trade Marks Act (TMA) introduced in 1994. For the purpose of fashion companies, where new design ranges often change extremely rapidly, it may, in fact, be more advantageous to establish a strong brand name identity. While numerous and diverse design ranges may be launched and marketed throughout the year, a consistent and comprehensive brand identity can effectively assist in building up the fashion companies' ongoing reputation amongst consumers.

Trade marks principally act as identification symbols, or words used in the course of trading, to indicate the connection between a certain company and the products sold by the organisation, distinguishing one company's goods from other competitive traders and essentially providing protection for the goodwill and reputation of a firm through its products.[11] By protecting and supporting a successful trade mark, owners will help to maintain and possibly even increase their market share.

In the mind of the consumer the trade mark can help to differentiate the product range and make it stand out amongst the multitude of other fashion brands available in the market-place. Using the trade mark effectively to gain market share and protecting it with fierce vigilance can help to imply a warning to competitors that the same attitude will be applied for designs, thereby making them think twice before producing counterfeit products.

In researching the subject of trade marks, publications and field specialists often refer to trade marks as being the single most valuable marketing tool a company could have. Nevertheless it is also true that 'the level of protection offered via trade marks is seriously underestimated by the fashion industry'.

The general lack of knowledge and appreciation of trade mark legislation may be explained by the fact that until the new Trade Mark Act in 1994, intellectual property rights for brands were regulated by a rather out-of-date and complex trade marks law dating back to *1938*.

However, the long-awaited TMA 1994 has considerably improved the trade mark protection facilities available to businesses and individuals and was well received from day one when the Registry received more than 1,000 applications within hours of the new legislation coming into force.

An example of the strength a trade mark can achieve is the 'Lycra' brand name used by Du Pont for its elastane fibre. During the 1980s and 1990s the trade mark has gone from strength to strength for apparel categories such as hosiery, swimwear, body wear and a wide range of sportswear reaching consumer awareness levels as high as 85%. To remind consumers that the Lycra brand is only supplied by Du Pont, branding was updated in the early 1990s to read 'Lycra—*only* by Du Pont'.

The company has marketed the trade mark so successfully that for some consumer groups it is the ultimate brand name for quality stretch clothing. Not surprisingly one part of the brand's promotion campaign included the text *'For millions of consumers two words will describe a thousand feelings—Lycra Sensations'* supported by visual examples of the many applications for the branded fibre such as swimwear, tights, sportswear, woven and tailored garments as well as lingerie. Another example of the promotion of the branded fibre is seen in Figure 5.1.

Trade Marks Act 1994

The start to introducing up-to-date trade mark legislation for effective business application took shape during 1993–4 when the UK legislature passed a new Trade Marks Bill aiming to close existing legal loopholes and implement the foundations for European harmonisation. The case for improvement was highlighted by a number of trading standards disputes

CASE STUDY

Trading standards case study

A court case initiated by Kent trading standards officers, against a market trader selling counterfeit T-shirts led to the trader evading prosecution on the basis that by having advertised on cardboard signs that the garments were 'brand copies' of Fila, Levi's, Adidas, Puma and Reebok, selling for the fractional price of £1.99.

A High Court appeal upheld that the market trader under the Trades Description Act, having correctly described the goods as 'copies' had not misled customers or broken the existing law.

Following this ruling a dramatically large number of traders started to display 'brand copies' disclaimer notices. With markets opening up to bootleggers and counterfeiters giving manufacturers and copycat suppliers a ready outlet for their copy goods.

---

whereby market traders claimed to deal legally in counterfeit goods shown in the case study above.

The new Trade Marks Act came into force on October 31, 1994, with

Shape up your sweaters and knits?

Happy to help.

Freedom of movement for your suits and skirts?

Go right ahead.

Breathe more life into your sportswear?

Delighted if you do.

Put more comfort in your underwear line?

Fine with us.

Looking for hosiery that feels and fits better?

Be our guest.

Want your swimwear to stay smarter longer?

No problem.

Abuse our trademark?

See you in court.

If you are using LYCRA® in your products and you're not sure how to advertise the fact, call us.

And if you're using another elastane and *calling* it "Lycra" you'd better also call your lawyer. Because the next time you see us it'll be in court.

When you use LYCRA®, it really pays to tell your customers about it. By adding our hang-tag or label to your garments, or our logo to your packaging or advertising, you are also adding the quality and performance reassurance of one of the world's best-known, most-valued brand names — a name that DuPont has actively and successfully promoted for more than two decades.

You already know the comfort, fit and freedom of movement that LYCRA® can bring. So if you're using it, it makes good marketing sense to use our trademark too.

But if you're not, don't even think about it.

LYCRA®
ONLY BY DUPONT

® LYCRA is a registered trademark of DuPont

Figure 5.1 Trade mark success 'Lycra only by Du Pont'—advertising warning against imitation fibres. Reproduced with the permission of Du Pont De Nemours International SA © 1996

the general effect of making it easier for trade mark users in the UK to register a much wider range of marks through simplified registration and improved protection procedures. The field of infringement rights has also been considerably improved by extending the infringement protection to include use of the same or *similar marks on similar goods*. Even further protection is provided for well-known registered trade marks which are considered infringed by use of the same or *similar* mark on totally *dissimilar* goods on the grounds of the likelihood of confusing the public.

One very important new element of the legislation is the definition of what constitutes and qualifies as a 'trade mark'. According to the new 1994 Act a trade mark can consist of any sign capable of being graphically presented and which is capable of distinguishing goods or services of one undertaking from those of others.

Apart from the mark itself (be it a word, symbol or possibly an advertising slogan), protection also includes '*shapes*' of goods or their packaging, *colours* and even *sounds* or *smells*. Provided these brand elements are distinctive and can be represented graphically (or be clearly described, e.g. in the case of a perfume scent), they may qualify to be registered as trade marks.

Typical examples of 'shapes' include the Coca-Cola bottle and the Jif Lemon container, which in the past have been subjects of major 'passing off' cases. Other branded products that have made use of the new trade mark definition include perfume products such as 'Chanel No. 5', where clear description of the distinctive scent now can register as part of the trade mark. Note that in interpreting the trade mark element of 'shape' the mark cannot be registered if it consists *exclusively* of:

- the shape which results from the nature of the goods themselves;
- the shape of goods necessary to obtain a technical result;
- the shape which gives substantial value to the goods.

The new Trade Marks Act has been welcomed by a number of industries and organisations concerned with design and branded products. Apart from the wider trade mark protection it is also felt that the new protection system will improve and challenge both companies and designers to produce more original trade marks/logos, that are distinctive enough to obtain trade mark registration and strong enough to protect against brand imitations. At the same time creators will now have to be very careful not to copy other companies' or individuals' trade mark designs and logos, however inadvertently.

CASE STUDY

Infringement of the packaging shape

Reports in 1995 brought to light an infringement dispute of a distinctive T-shirt packaging used—and trade mark registered—by a British clothing company. The distinctive concept of vacuum packing garments was due to be introduced in the UK by a European retail chain. However, the British design company claimed that the carriers resembled their own trade mark registered wrapping too closely and would cause public confusion of the British and European brands. As a result the overseas retail chain acted by surrendering the packaging and apologising, claiming the resemblance was a mistake.

*   **Comment:** the successful outcome for the British company is a clear example of the wider spanning trade mark protection available under the 1994 Trade Marks Act, and should in many cases help to encourage companies developing their trade mark further. In the past the 'trade mark' concept for many fashion companies has been thought of as 'a name' and 'a logo'. Whereas with the improved trade mark protection, more lateral thinking and new ways of interpreting the trade mark concept and its opportunities could assist in taking full advantage of the broader protection now available through trade mark elements such as 'shape', 'colour', 'sound' and possibly even 'smell', thereby developing much more sophisticated trade marks and brand logos.*

To register or not to register?

Registration of a trade mark is not compulsory in the UK but without registration an owner cannot bring an action of infringement to protect the mark, although a common law action for 'passing off' a company's unregistered trade mark may be initiated. To assess the strengths, weaknesses and possible risks of such legal action based on an unregistered trade mark, the advice of at least one legal specialist should be taken, to ensure there is a case to answer for the alleged infringer.

Suing for infringement of a *registered* mark is much simpler and faster. This is because in infringement proceedings, trade mark users can base their case simply upon the certificate of registration. Whereas in 'passing off' proceedings involving unregistered trade marks, owners only succeed if they can demonstrate to the court that they have established a reputation with their trade mark, and that an accused trader, by using the same mark, is likely to confuse or deceive the public.[9]

Registration, on the other hand, gives an immediate right to prevent someone using the same trade mark, generally *without* the need to prove business reputation or demonstrate a risk of confusion between the trade marks in question. It is therefore advisable whenever possible to register the trade mark name and logo plus any distinctive product elements which may qualify as the trade mark. Also, it should be considered that legislation both in the UK and on a European level for Community trade marks, now grants primary protection for the first *registered* trade mark compared to the unregistered 'first use' claim of a brand.

Wherever the trade mark appears on garments or in advertising materials the company should ensure it makes use of the small ™ symbol to remind competitors and possible counterfeiters that the name and/or logo is a trade mark. *If* the mark is protected via trade mark registration the international ® symbol can be used to reinforce the message that intellectual property rights are claimed. However, under no circumstances should the ® symbol be wrongfully applied to goods which are *not registered* as the misuse can lead to criminal sanctions.

Criteria and rights for trade mark registration

The brand name/trade mark can be an invented or an ordinary word used in a non-literal way (e.g. 'Apple' for a computer). A trade mark must not be likely to confuse or deceive the public about the nature of the goods and their quality, or conflict with a trade mark already registered for similar or dissimilar product categories.

Where a trade mark is already registered for quite different products than textiles or clothing, e.g. food and drink products, the existing registration holder must give its permission before the trade mark can be registered for clothing and fashion products. If the trade mark owner of the dissimilar goods decides that the new registration for any reason will be detrimental, the new trade mark registration can be rejected. Alternatively, *should* the earlier registration owner consent to the new registration for the different product classes the application can go ahead, unless the Registrar finds it likely that the new registration might possibly deceive the public.

In general, a trade mark should not conflict with existing marks already used by other businesses or individuals. An example would be the similarities between two brand names such as 'Jonelle' and 'Joelle'. A similar trade mark confusion could arise when comparing the jeans wear brands 'Levi's Jeans' and 'Evis Genes', hence the latter, Japanese and very up-market designer brand is marketed with the brand name 'Evisu'.

Note that when carrying out searches to establish if the mark exists as an 'earlier mark', the definition of 'existing' is not merely concerned with marks registered in the UK register but also includes European Community trade marks or an international trade mark which has effect in the United Kingdom via international agreements.

Distinctiveness of the trade mark

As the protection basis for a registered trade mark is a statutory monopoly for the registration owner, words and/or symbols which other traders are likely to use in their normal conduct of trading or which may obstruct/restrict normal business cannot be accepted by the Registrar, unless it can be established that the applicant, through extensive use of the trade mark, has clearly established the mark itself as distinctive in the market-place.

Before the TMA 1994, some types of marks were automatically excluded from obtaining registration. Typically these excluded marks were:

- names of individuals, companies or firms, unless represented in highly stylised form;
- surnames, unless very rare;
- nearly all geographical names;
- words deceptive of the product character or quality.

However, under the new Act of 1994 the above categories may in some cases be able to qualify as registered marks, provided that it can be established that the mark has in fact become recognised as a company's mark for its goods or services.

Some mark categories which generally continue to be insufficiently distinctive for registration purposes include signs or indications describing the product kind, quality, quantity, intended purpose, value, geographic origin, time of production or other characteristics of goods, plus any words or signs commonly used in the trade or current language. However, all of these trade mark categories, normally exempt from registration, may be registered provided it can be demonstrated that before the date of application for registration, the mark has in fact acquired a distinctive character as a result of the use made of it.[10]

Categories of marks which remain unregistrable as trade marks include national emblems, such as flags and royal arms or signs indicating patronage.

Classification of registered trade marks

To try and ensure that trade mark registration strikes a balance of not becoming prohibitive throughout all industries, an application must specify the goods that the mark will be used in connection with. If registration is sought for several product classes, under the TMA 1994, only one application is filed for all product types, as opposed to the 'old' law where individual applications had to be made for each single 'class' one was seeking registration for. The new system of 'one application for all registration classes' is a considerable improvement for applicants, reducing the time and cost factors for filing a trade mark registration.

The classification list for goods and services, currently used for UK trade mark registration has no fewer than 42 product/service classes, covering areas ranging from scientific, medical and financial industries to agriculture, education and food and drink. Trade mark classes most applicable for the clothing and textile industries are:

- Class 18: leather and imitations of leather and goods made of these materials.
- Class 22: raw fibrous textile materials and padding materials.
- Class 23: yarns and threads, for textile use.
- Class 24: textiles and textile piece goods not included in other classes.
- Class 25: clothing, footwear and headgear.
- Class 26: lace, embroidery and mainly dressmakers' articles such as buttons, hooks and eyes, pins and needles.

In stating the trade mark classes for which registration is sought, the important aspect is to fully specify the goods within each product class in order to define the trade mark monopoly for the particular goods.

Registration procedure

The trade mark registration procedure takes on a similar system as that of patent and registered design applications. Firstly, the application for registration (Form TM No. 3) is filed at the Trade Marks Registry—a branch of the Patent Office. The application is then examined to ensure the trade mark is distinctive, not deceptive and does not conflict with existing registered trade marks. If objections are raised by the examiner the applicant may argue its case in writing or at an oral hearing before a senior official at the Trade Marks Registry.

In order to avoid unnecessary complications, delays or extra costs incurred from incomplete/incorrect applications, trade mark owners should make use of a professional trade mark agent (refer to Address List for official organisations).

Priority dates can be claimed for the same trade mark filed in any membership country of the Paris Convention for Protection of Industrial Property as long as the application claiming a priority date is filed within the first six months of the original UK registration date. Any priority claim must relate to the same mark and same product classes.

When a trade mark is accepted for registration, it is advertised in the *Trade Marks Journal* to allow others to oppose registration. If there is no opposition, the trade mark is then entered on the Register.[9]

The trade mark application form itself consists of two A4 pages plus two additional pages for listing the registration classes and description of the articles which fall within each class. Official forms are available from the Trade Marks Registry, together with explanatory leaflets and the list of fees for various application types.

The information fields to be completed on the application are as follows:

1. your trade mark reference;
2. representation of the mark—shown graphically (8 × 8 cm/max. A4 format) and clear description of additional trade mark elements (shape/colour/smell);
3. indicate if the mark is not a word or picture (i.e. three-dimensional);
4. indicate the number of marks in the series (if applicable);
5. priority date(s) claimed if any (date, country and application number);
6. specification of trade mark classes and list of goods;
7. details of applicant—full name and address details;
8. name of agent (if appropriate);
9. state if the trade mark application is for (a) a certification trade mark or (b) a collective trade mark;
10. indicate any disclaimers and limitations (i.e. trade mark colour).

Finally, sign and date the application to confirm ownership or owner's consent for filing the trade mark application.

Source: The Patent Office/Trade Mark Registry, UK

Once the application is fully processed and registration granted, the applicant will receive the official Certificate of Registration. The official registration date for a successful application will be the initial filing date or the date of priority claim if any is applicable to the trade mark.

Throughout the application procedures the trade mark owner is allowed the opportunity to carry out minor application corrections, amendments or to state his case if opposition for registration of the mark occurs.

Certification and collective trade marks

A *certification trade mark* is used to certify that goods carrying the mark are produced according to certain specifications, processes, quality levels or material content.

The certification mark is registered in a similar fashion as other trade mark applications and confers the same exclusive rights. The owner of the certification mark must, in addition to the standard application, also supply the registry with the regulations governing the certification mark. The Registrar must be satisfied that the certification owner is sufficiently competent to operate the proposed certification procedures and regulations satisfactorily—for anyone whose goods qualify for the mark—before the registration is granted to the certifying body or individual owner.

Examples of certification trade marks from the fashion industry include the well-known Wool Mark with certification marks 'Pure New Wool' and 'Wool Rich Blend' (see following Example), while the oldest surviving British certification trade mark, known worldwide for its superior quality is the 'Harris Tweed' certification trade mark registered in the UK since 1905.

HAND WOVEN

Harris Tweed

Certification Trade Mark

The mark of quality the world over.

PUBLISHED BY THE HARRIS TWEED ASSOCIATION LTD.

'Harris Tweed means a tweed made from pure virgin wool produced in Scotland, spun, dyed and finished in the Outer Hebrides and hand woven by the islanders in their own homes in the islands of Lewis, Harris, Uist, Barra and their several purtenances and all known as the Outer Hebrides' *The Harris Tweed Authority*. The 'Harris Tweed Authority' is the statutory body and the *only* authority which can certify Harris Tweed textiles. The role of the Authority is that of custodian of the 'Orb and Cross' Certification Trade Mark. It monitors the processes in the making of Harris Tweed including hand-weaving, authenticates, certifies and stamps Harris Tweed, protects the industry and the trade mark internationally, promotes Harris Tweed in world markets and controls the issue of the Harris Tweed garment labels.

The Authority's main functions include:

1. promoting, maintaining and advertising the reputation and standard of quality of Harris Tweed;
2. registering, maintaining and defending trade marks and other property anywhere in the world;
3. preventing the possession and/or sale as 'Harris Tweed' of counterfeit goods.

The
Harris Tweed
Association Limited

Certification
Trade Mark

The 'Orb and Cross' certification trade mark is now registered in more than 33 countries and Harris Tweed fabrics are used by several well-known designers, e.g. Ally Capellino, Arabella Pollen, Vivienne Westwood and Joe Casely Hayford.

Reproduced with the permission of The Harris Tweed Authority, Isle of Lewis, UK

Collective marks represent a trade mark category which was introduced for the first time in the 1994 Act and which is available for registration by business organisations who authorise the use of marks or symbols for members to display their association. This trade mark category has all the characteristics of an ordinary mark and uses the same application structure as for certification marks. The applicant for a collective mark must, in addition to the standard application form, supply a copy of the regulations

EXAMPLE

Certification trade marks

WOOLMARK   WOOLBLENDMARK

CERTIFICATION TRADE MARK   CERTIFICATION TRADE MARK
PURE NEW WOOL   WOOL RICH BLEND

'*The Woolmark (Woolblendmark), the symbol of Pure New Wool (Wool Rich Blend) products, are the Trade Marks owned by IWS and may only be used by licensed manufacturers on products meeting appropriate performance specifications.*' *(IWS).*

The Woolmark

The Woolmark is a registered trade mark owned by the International Wool Secretariat (IWS). It is registered in more than 140 countries and is currently used by licensed manufacturers in more than 60 countries on a wide range of textile products, including knitwear, outerwear, underwear, carpets, upholstery and blankets.

The Woolmark was introduced in 1964 to identify products made from pure new wool which meet strict quality standards. The quality standards cover a wide range of attributes including colour fastness, abrasion, resistance, seam slippage, machine washability and fabric strength in addition to fibre content.

The Woolmark can only be used by manufacturers who have been licensed by IWS and whose products confirm to IWS standards. Licensed manufacturers are fully responsible for meeting the IWS specifications and for maintaining strict levels of in-house quality control. Through its own laboratories, IWS carries out an extensive programme of quality control monitoring to ensure that Woolmark standards are being maintained. Licensed manufacturers who produce Woolmark merchandise below the specified quality standards risk losing their licences.

Since it was launched 30 years ago the Woolmark has been widely promoted and is now one of the most universally recognised textile symbols.

Reproduced with the permission of IWS, © 1996

to be used for authorising the collective mark (within nine months of filing the application).[10]

Cost and time factors

The complete application process, including examination of registrability and any possible conflict with other marks on average may take about two years from the date of filing of the application. If necessary priority processing of the application may be requested.

Before starting to prepare the official application, it is advisable to carry out preliminary searches both via official registry sources and within general business and commerce, to avoid the time and cost consuming exercise of filing an application only to find the mark has already been registered or an unregistered mark later disputes the registration. Also, as the application is a formal and legal procedure it is worth taking the advice and assistance of an expert to ensure the application is as complete as possible and does not at a later stage become subject to interpretation or variation by competitors or individuals. The cost arising from a trade mark agent consists of both fixed and time-based fees, general guidelines of cost can be obtained by contacting the local agent or agent organisations directly (refer to Address List for contact organisations).

As a guideline, the standard cost of a trade mark application, made on Form TM3 is currently £225 (subject to annual adjustment) for one product classification plus a further £125 per class for each extra product. The initial registration is valid for 10 years, whereafter it can be renewed at regular intervals every 10 years at a cost of approximately £250 for one class and £200 for each additional class (using 'Form TM11').

Since the introduction of the new Trade Marks Act, marks must be used for goods or services on a continuing basis. This will in return avoid the situation of companies maintaining trade mark registrations purely as a means of restricting business competition. Any registered mark not used for a period of five years can, upon application from a third party, be revoked on the grounds of non-use—unless the trade mark owner can prove the opposite.

Trade mark licensing

Trade mark licensing predating 1994 was strictly controlled and restricted by the legislation from 1938. The ownership conditions of a registered trade mark are now greatly improved for registration holders who can grant licences as they see fit for their individual business although it remains the responsibility of the trade mark proprietor to ensure licensees do not misuse the mark or render it invalid, by applying the trade mark to product categories for which the brand/logo has not been officially registered or onto types of goods not included in the parties' licence agreement. Also, a trade mark owner should remember that it is in his business interest to monitor the licensed product range on a continuing basis, in relation to, e.g. general quality control and new product development/prototypes, thereby ensuring that the licensed products meet the same quality, perceived value and performance as the original branded products.

Licensing may take place in various forms—by granting a licence for *all* product categories registered or for specific goods only. Under the new structure of the legislation it becomes possible to give licensees rights to contract sub-licensees and for licence holders to bring legal action against trade mark infringements.

Also, the exclusive licence may be negotiated for trade mark classes only to be produced by the new licence holder. Any such agreements may be filed and recorded with the Trade Mark Registry using Form TM50 (approximate fee £50). Note, however, that if such licences are *not* filed, the rights granted to licensees by the trade mark owner are not enforceable against any third party infringing the licensed rights. This is also the case when any person through assignment or transfer of ownership rights becomes entitled to a registered trade mark. To register, the entitlement Form TM16 is filed with the Registry, together with the current fee.

Whereas previously licence agreement applications (known as registered user agreements) were subject to detailed scrutiny, under the Trade Marks Act 1994 this scrutinising examination system has been abolished, allowing the trade mark owner much greater freedom to regulate the trade mark asset. Instead, the Registrar is now obliged to accept and register the application/notification of a licensee or assignment without raising any objections.

However, it is vital for the licensee to ensure a licence notification is logged with the Trade Mark Registry right from the start of the licensing agreement to ensure the licensee is not exposed to having to deal with any licence infringement *without the protection rights* of the trade mark owner. Also, without filing the registered user notification, the licensee risks being legally denied any financial remedies against the infringement.

Registered trade marks for the fashion industry

There is great scope for distinctive trade marks in the brand oriented fashion industry, via trade mark exploitation and brand extension where product and brand franchising is based on licensing of registered trade marks, whilst brand extension can be achieved by brand licensing into other product categories, e.g. fashion accessories.

A key element to successful licensing operations is the ability to stop pirating and imitations of the brand. To achieve this, trade mark registration is an indispensable protection weapon against counterfeit products.

Another aspect to consider is that within the fashion industries a majority of businesses use their brand names and trade marks to build upon and strengthen their identity in the market-place from season to season. Consider for example what effect it would have for any fashion company to drop their brand name from one day to the next?

Recent trends in the 1990s for the clothing and footwear industries, indicate a growing number of well-established and successful specialist brands diversifying into offering more comprehensive product ranges in order to fully benefit from the strength of their brand name. Examples include:

- *Pringle*—initially known for knitwear, launched an extensive clothing range for the 1994 spring/summer season.
- *Dr. Martens*—famous for its boots, branching into branded casual wear.
- *Burberrys*—predominantly known for their raincoats, expanding with evening wear and jewellery ranges.
- *Paul Smith*—originally a menswear brand now includes children's and women's wear collections.
- *Benetton*—already an established lifestyle brand, diversifying with the launch of swimwear, underwear and sleep wear.

Licensing agreements between designers and large manufacturers and retailers have also become an option for small-scale couture designers to benefit from their designer name and increase business profitability. Such links in the United Kingdom have been seen amongst brands like Antony Price and Ariella, Bella Freud and Michael Ross, Katharine Hamnett and Nancy Vale plus Nicholas Knightly linked with Cutler and Gross.

Returning to the example of the branded fibre trade mark 'Lycra—only by Du Pont', this is a trade mark which has clearly established the brand extremely well through consumer awareness campaigns, brand certification procedures both for textile and garment producers and generally promoting the fibre's superior performance qualities both within the fashion industry and directly to consumers.

Initially the branded fibre was introduced for stretch garments such as leggings, leotards and swimwear products, followed by brand extension to include product categories such as lace, heavy knitwear and tailored clothing in woven material. Supporting the garments' promotion at retail level via special ticketing programmes such as that shown in Figure 5.2.

The supply of garment swing tickets and fabric testing to confirm content of the branded fibre are both available without charge to manufacturers. The 'Lycra' fabric testing carried out by the trade mark owner also helps to identify possible counterfeit sources.

In response to trade mark infringements of the branded elastane fibre, 1997 will see the introduction of a formal licensing system (initially for hosiery producers only)—in an attempt to stamp out brand infringements and products using Lycra® elastane in minor quantities insufficient to fulfil the performance expected of the branded fibre.

New LYCRA® Swing Tickets
The difference is LYCRA®

Figure 5.2 Registered trade mark promotion at retail level: brand labelling and swing promotion. Reproduced with the permission of Du Pont De Nemours International SA © 1996

CASE STUDY

Lycra® Trade mark infringement (1995)

In the clothing industry companies will often source fabric outside the United Kingdom, however, the following example illustrates how in one instance the garment producer suddenly found himself entangled in a trade mark infringement.

On numerous occasions fabric had been sourced abroad for a high quality sportswear range marketed in the UK. For a range where special dye techniques would be applied to the finished garments a fabric was sourced from a European country which was sufficiently heavy for the purpose as well as being reasonably priced. One of the fabric specifications was for the fabric to contain Lycra® elastane for quality reasons and the clothing producer therefore accepted the price point would be higher compared to unbranded elastane.

Alas, the fabric arrived 'just in time' for the pre-booked production slot—all documents stating 'Cotton/Lycra' and also the fabric handle, stretch and weight appeared to be correct. The fabric continued to be converted into garments. At the same time the required sample of production fabric was sent for Lycra fibre verification with the UK trade mark owner, in order to receive the Lycra promotion tickets for the range.

However, the fibre verification test showed the fabric did clearly not contain the branded fibre and the garment producer had in fact been sold a counterfeit 'Lycra' material. Although the UK manufacturer could prove to the trade mark owner, through invoice documentation, that they had been seriously misled by both the fabric producer and all relevant documentation, several additional costs had to be meet through relabelling and processing of all garments, withdrawal of the Lycra® sales point and general price reduction as the range could not benefit from promotion of the branded fibre.

The licence agreements will be beneficial in making it easier and less time-consuming to take legal action against trade mark counterfeiters throughout Europe. The licensing procedure—relating to the specification standards of hosiery products and how the Lycra® fibre is put into the garment—is viewed positively by major producers and multiple retailers whose general opinion is that the 'Lycra' logo already stands for quality and any measures taken to ensure standards are met are commendable.

The financial importance of protecting a successful trade mark and brand name is illustrated by the drastic actions taken by companies trying to protect trade mark ownership when their brand is exposed to misuse or imitation by competitors.

CASE STUDY

Active Inc. versus Slix Swimwear

In autumn 1990 retailers selling the swimwear range 'Activ' by Slix received letters directly from the company Active Inc., stating that as proprietor of the registered trade mark 'Active' (no. 1288255) Active Inc. was taking 'court action against swimwear maker Slix, to prevent its use of the unregistered mark "Activ by Slix" . . . '. The letter continued that should the defendant lose the legal case 'retailers cannot legally sell stock bearing the words "Activ by Slix" . . . '. The retail reaction was to contact the Slix company asking for an explanation.

Although legal advice to the Slix organisation found the company to be in the clear, the letters sent to retailers alleging an infringement produced a strong reaction from retailers, confirmed by the Slix sales director: 'They (the retailers) are not unduly worried once they know what it is all about'.

Trade Mark dispute Active vs. Activ

The 'Activ by Slix' swimwear collection, had been launched three years prior to the dispute, designed to differentiate between the company's traditional fashion swimwear and a more sporty competition style range also by Slix.

The last details published for this case were that Slix was considering the different options of action which could be taken. Whilst the viewpoint of Active Inc., owner of the registered trade mark 'Active' was that 'It took the company 4 years to get its registered trade mark and unless we protect it we will lose it'.

Reproduced by permission of Drapers Record © November 17, 1990, illustration reproduced with the permission of Slix Ltd (under new company management)

The final outcome of the dispute 'Active' Inc. vs. 'Activ by Slix' was not published to the industry and settlement may have taken place out of court. However, some of the issues to consider in this case are:

1. *Active was a registered trade mark owned by Active Inc., and by law has monopoly for producing, and selling the goods covered by its registration (i.e. swimwear) under its trade mark. It can also prevent other companies using similar trade marks for the same type of product if the consumers are likely to be confused by the similarities.*

2. *At the same time the Slix organisation may argue that the 'Activ by Slix' range has been sold for three years and in its own right achieved recognition and reputation. However, if Active Inc. throughout this period of time held a registration of the trade mark Active, the registered brand name will legally stand stronger than the unregistered brand.*

CASE STUDY

'Passing off' dispute of the Puffa brand (1993)

Puffa, the company whose padded jackets have become synonymous with the country set, served in 1993 one of the UK's largest retail chains with a High Court writ. The alleged trade mark infringement was based on the allegation that a multiple retailer was seen to be 'passing off' its own goods by using the description 'puffa jackets' in its customer magazine for box quilted garments of similar appearance to those manufactured and marketed under the 'Puffa' brand name.

In the writ Puffa was seeking damages and an injunction barring the multiple retailer from trading in the alleged products. The initial response from the retail chain in this instance was to dispute the claim. Presumably the dispute was finally settled by the parties out of court, as no further court actions were published by either companies.

Reproduced with the permission of Puffa Ltd © 1996

Summary of registered protection rights

There are certain formalities and requirements involved in obtaining registered protection which are covered in this chapter. Apart from the direct cost of preparing documents and design representations, it must be remembered that in most instances, legal assistance will be required to ensure the predominantly written registration will be legally 'watertight' with no loopholes for potential copyright infringement.

The product elements which are protected by each registration category have been clearly defined by current UK legislation—ranging from strictly functional concepts for patents to aesthetic aspects of a product design protected via registered design.

In relation to registered design, the intellectual proprietor(s) should not only consider the registration costs or direct expenses but also be clear about the actual requirements of the business and the purpose of registering the design, be it to exercise monopoly of a new design concept, enable licensing and/or to protect the existing as well as long-term trading environment or future business fields via product/brand diversification.

The latest Trade Marks Act introduced in 1994 offers much wider protection and improved enforcement rights for brand name and logos which is vital in the environment of competitive fashion industries. On the basis that while the product ranges of fashion change from season to season, brand name and trade marks are viewed as the continuing asset upon which business is built in the long term, also considering that the majority of the industry is trading in markets where strong brand loyalty exists.

The definition of a trade mark, under the TMA 1994, now spans more widely than merely covering the brand name and logo. It can also cover product elements such as 'shape', 'colour' and perhaps less applicable for fashion products 'sound' and 'smell'.

6

HOW TO DEAL WITH DESIGN INFRINGEMENT

6.1 How to deal with design infringement

The subject of design infringement and copying of intellectual property is a highly sensitive matter which many businesses are most reluctant to draw any attention to, primarily, due to the concern that publicity regarding infringements might boost the sales of copies or severely damage the company's image and brand name. Industry sources confirm that this unwillingness to discuss any information related to allegations of copying and design protection in general is often caused particularly by larger organisations who 'simply hate any publicity which may damage future business'. Although one positive result of such an anti-PR standpoint is that the majority of design and copyright disputes are settled out of court to avoid damaging PR and to save the time and cost involved in full-blown court cases. However, for the same reason case studies illustrating the issues of dealing with infringement of intellectual property are, to a certain degree, inaccessible to the public and limited to issues raised in the trade press or company press releases.

For smaller companies, a major consideration when deciding to take action against infringement, is the risk of inflicting large-scale litigation costs. Wherever the exercise of legal rights is involved, this is of course always a possibility. But in the incidence of intellectual property litigation, only a very small proportion of cases actually reach the courts and a number of alternative means exist to prevent or solve the problem of counterfeiting and unauthorised copying.

In addition to this, it is possible to *insure* all forms of intellectual property rights against the costs of a lawsuit, if the relevant application were to be prosecuted by a qualified practitioner such as a patent agent or trade mark agent. The option of IP insurance policies should be balanced with the finding that although in the UK legal costs are paid to the successful litigant by the loser, the actual amount recovered is unlikely to exceed 65–75% of the cost expended and always *subject to the defendant's liquidity*. And while legal insurance can often alleviate financial pressures, it is always advisable to judge the cost of proceeding with a case against the expected outcome—**'Balance the risk, cost and gain'**.[3]

Whatever you decide to do always make the decision on purely commercial grounds by assessing the benefits against possible risk and overall cost factors. It is dangerous and can prove excessively costly to make decisions for emotional reasons or 'as a matter of principle'.

One golden rule to follow when discovering infringement of protected intellectual property rights is to take legal advice from a specialist agent or solicitor immediately. This will allow for any issues involved to be assessed in a legal context. Because the design proprietor or creator will often experience the copying literally as personal theft, it is important to obtain qualified advice to balance the alleged infringement objectively and as it would be viewed under current legislation.

In particular, one should, under no circumstances, write or speak to the other company—especially as it is unlawful to issue unjustified threats against an alleged infringer. And although notification that a given design is protected does not constitute threatening proceedings, exactly what constitutes an 'unjustified threat' in law is not always easy for a lay person to decide.[11] Even in cases where legal advice *is* taken successful litigation is no guarantee because of the various legal complexities of intellectual property which may affect the outcome of a dispute. In that connection one UK dispute which comes to mind—where litigation action proceeded following legal advice—is a tie-dye swimwear dispute which received a great deal of publicity in the national UK press.

Before taking any form of legal action against a company or individual alleged to have infringed intellectual property rights, be aware that if your ownership rights in any way have become invalid or expired, threats of litigation to 'scare off' business competitors could risk legal counter-action for damages, an injunction and/or a declaration that the allegations made were unfounded. Following the introduction of the Trade Marks Act 1994 and in line with patent and design legislation, any person exposed to groundless threats of infringement litigation can bring a

CASE STUDY

A dispute of the textile design's ownership? The tie–dye swimwear range (1995–97)

The dispute was between a small size design company trading in exclusive, up-market women's wear claiming design infringement against one of Britain's largest multiple retailers. The case focused on a swimwear range using brightly coloured tie-dye fabric with the designer's branded garments retailing in excess of £100. In comparison, costumes in a similar fabric were sold by the retail chain accused of copying the exclusive designer range, retailing at much lower high street prices of approximately £25.

To help illustrate the designer's contention that her rights had been abused, photographs published in the press showed models wearing the 'original' swimwear versus the alleged 'copy' garments in question. However, upon studying the photographic illustrations both tie-dye ranges appeared to consist of quite commonplace designs including scoop-neck, sleeveless or crew neck, short sleeve leotards. And on this basis one might argue that the creative element of the swimwear range consisted perhaps not so much of the garment designs and styling, but to a much larger degree was achieved through the element of strong colour combination and the distinct tie-dye effect of the fabric.

In which case, the similarities of the swimwear ranges lay not in the ownership of the garments' 'design', defined in legal terms as relating only to 'shape and/or configuration', indeed posing the question if there was any legal basis for design protection.

On the other hand if the designer was to claim exclusivity and copyright of the fabric's tie-dye effect it would be questioned if the tie-dye effect indeed was created by the designer brand or purchased for exclusive use by the designer's firm. Or was the tie-dye effect part of a textile supplier's standard fabric processes, available without exclusive rights to a wide number of clothing producers? As a matter of interest other sports/swimwear clothing companies in the UK industry were offered closely identical tie-dye colour schemes as a standard process apparently owned by a dye house specialist.

In which case it may indicate that when the exclusive design company took legal action alleging copying by the multiple retailer, some of the above textile/tie-dye ownership factors and their legal implications may not have been fully assessed before the decision was made to proceed with further action, resulting in the firm stand by the multiple retailer expressing that the designer's copying claim 'had no substance'.

The dispute and allegations of design infringement concluded in January 1997 when, on the retailer's application to the High Court, the case was struck out.

'threats action' as a remedy against the unjustified litigation threat. Therefore when becoming aware of possible infringement, professional assistance should be taken to ensure no allegations are made which constitute 'unjustified threats'. Generally this will mean the preparation of letters by a legal professional before action is taken further.

Conversely, when being threatened with litigation do not panic. In many instances it will be possible to reach mutual agreement whereby both parties benefit commercially and financially, even when despite the best efforts to avoid infringement of others' rights it is found that there *is* full justification for the complaint.[11]

Where infringement takes place without the infringer realising that the original design benefits from copyright protection, it is recommended that (*subject* to measures to protect the proprietor's legal position should the matter not be settled amicably) the infringer is given notice of the ownership claim and allowed the opportunity to remedy the situation by withdrawing the offending design and possibly offering compensation. The notification that copyright of an original design is being illegally invaded will also remove the opportunity of the infringer claiming later that he was innocent of knowingly breaking any copyright ownership. (Refer to case studies and examples in Chapters 3 and 4).

In cases where the source of infringement is known, notification of the ownership claim can be made directly to the infringer. However, if the copying parties cannot be located, a public advertisement in a trade publication can be used to advise of the intellectual property rights being claimed, as illustrated in this example:

> Highness Design' Ltd (proxy name) . . . wish it to be known that they will not tolerate any infringement of their copyrights or other design rights in the designs for their garments, and will not hesitate to institute legal proceedings against any person or company who infringes their rights (followed by proprietor/claimant(s) details).

Apart from the legal advice available from lawyers specialising in intellectual property legislation, a number of independent organisations specialise in advising members in cases of dispute and general copyright queries (see Address List). The points in Box 6.1 indicate some of the general recommendations given for fashion companies in the event of potential infringement.

In addition to the list of action points, it is also worth keeping in mind that often a retailer's contract will incorporate an infringement clause

---

Box 6.1

Practical action list in the event of potential infringement

These are some of the practical guidelines drawn up by the organisation FDPA. The advice outlines the initial action often required to be taken by the design right owner, to establish whether the intellectual property is exposed to infringement which can be pursued legally:

1. Acquire, preferably by purchasing, at least one example of the offending garment.
2. Keep a careful written record, including the sales receipt from where the offending garment was purchased and of anything that was said when the purchase was made.
3. Act immediately to place the matter before your legal advisers for opinion.
4. Assess the strengths and weaknesses of the case and any downsides!
5. No approach should be made to the infringer until qualified legal advice has been taken.

Note:
(a) In litigation cases, the following individuals will normally be required to give evidence: the designer, the purchaser of the infringing garment and the plaintiff's financial director/partner.
(b) Expert design evidence will invariably be required to convince the court that copying has been undertaken. Intellectual property organisations concerned with design protection such as the FDPA, will be able to assist with this aspect.
(c) Financial evidence will be required to sustain a claim of damages. This will often be given by a specialist in the calculation of such claims.

Reproduced with the permission of Achilleas Constantinou, Chairman of Fashion Design Protection Associates Ltd, © 1996 FDPA

---

concerning all intellectual property categories. Therefore in the event of any counterfeit allegations the buyer will be entitled to return all garments and products concerned to the supplier. Through the written contractual obligations (as well as being an implied condition of sale under the Sale of Goods Act) the supplier can also be made responsible for covering all losses, costs and damage claims experienced by the retail buyer. Therefore in many cases retail outlets can be found to be very co-operative in stopping the sales of copies although in other instances it may also be the retailers themselves who are infringing.

The vast majority of contracts issued by UK multiple retailers and store groups will include infringement clauses as part of the standard trading agreement between the buyer and supplier. But for many small–scale buyers and independent retailers issues such as payment terms and delivery often tend to be given priority, leaving the retail business unaware of its possible rights or responsibilities in cases of copyright disputes, or when faced with legal writs to block sales of alleged counterfeit products. As a result, the retailer could risk exposure to substantial financial losses if no contractual supplier obligations exist particularly when purchasing goods overseas where legal protection similar to the British Sale of Goods Act may not be in force. It is therefore in the greatest interest of businesses such as retailers, importers and wholesale operations to ensure that their contractual terms do not fail to state the suppliers' obligations and financial responsibility in connection with all issues relating to infringement and ownership claims made for intellectual property rights.

6.2 Remedies against counterfeit products

Before the introduction of current legislation through the Copyright, Designs and Patents Act 1988 and the Trade Marks Act 1994, it had been possible for the design proprietor to obtain 'conversion damages'. These were calculated by reference to the sale value of the infringing copies irrespective of the cost of producing the same. Such damages are no longer available and the principal commercial remedies have changed to focus on actions such as prohibitory injunctions and financial damage claims.

Interlocutory injunctions

In situations where immediate action is necessary to restrain the alleged infringement, application to the court can be made for an interlocutory injunction to halt production and sale of the alleged copies during the interim period up to a trial. The main purpose of such action is to avoid the situation worsening during the dispute. Before the court decides whether or not to grant the injunction the applicant will have to clearly state his case to convince the authorities, that *without* the injunction further damage will be caused to the IP proprietor financially or to the brand's reputation (see design right case study in section 4.2).

Although this remedy is the most commonly sought in disputes, it is not issued lightly and a special test based on balance of convenience is used to decide whether or not an injunction should be granted. The copyright owner must, at first sight, have a very strong case, partly because at the point of issuing an interlocutory injunction, all trial details may not have been fully examined. If, at a later trial, it becomes clear that the injunction should not have been granted, it will in fact be the plaintiff who will have to pay damages to the accused.

The undertaking to pay possible damages to the defendant is a prerequisite of the applicant obtaining an interlocutory injunction, pending the outcome of a full court hearing. On balance, it is worth noticing that in many cases it has been the experience that an injunction is often sufficient in halting further intellectual property infringement and the dispute can be settled between the parties involved.

Obtaining evidence via a court order

In some instances copyright holders will find counterfeiters or parties involved in their illegal business unwilling to release certain information to assist the investigation of alleged infringement. To force the co-operation of a company or individuals a court order may be sought to force the third party to produce evidence.

EXAMPLE

> In September 1994 a writ was issued to a Leicester-based company alleged to have dealt in Burberry counterfeit products. The trade mark owner alleged infringements of its trade mark, Burberry check and distinctive equestrian knight logo which had been reproduced on the counterfeit products. Although the wholesale/export company involved claimed that they thought the goods were genuine, the writ was issued after the wholesaler refused to disclose details of his supplier to the trade mark proprietor.

The 'Anton Piller' order

This type of court order is available in exceptional cases where there is a real risk and evidence that documents, materials or counterfeit products may be destroyed or moved to avoid prosecution. The court order will allow the plaintiff and any legal advisers access to the defendant's premises to search for and examine stock, documents and other evidence valuable for full litigation action.

This particular type of court order has been the subject of much criticism and as a result is highly regulated and only granted in very few cases.

Final injunction

Once the infringement is proven through trial, the court will generally grant a final restraining order preventing the accused party from producing any further copies or committing any other act of infringement. Also, it will be decided by the court what will happen to the copied garments, whether on request from the intellectual property owner the infringing goods and materials are handed over to the plaintiff. Alternatively the counterfeit goods may be ordered for destruction, to have all trade marks and branding removed from the items or a royalty may be awarded to the plaintiff.

Monetary claims

In cases where infringement is successfully proven the level of damages or other compensation can be calculated in a number of ways. One way is to base the claim on the profit which the defendant has made from the infringement. In other instances the claim may be based on the level of profit that would have been achieved by the plaintiff, had his company produced the garments. The underlying principle is that the intellectual property owner should be in no worse a position than he would have been had no infringement occurred.

If the level of damages cannot be proved, the court will generally award damages calculated upon an imaginary royalty basis. Where the infringer has acted flagrantly and made substantial profits from the infringement 'additional damages' may also be awarded to the rightful owner of the design or trade mark.

Action through the Criminal Justice Act

During the 1990s a drastic increase in crime has taken place, both in the United Kingdom and other European countries, whereby professional counterfeit operations of 'career criminals' are found dealing in vast quantities of counterfeit brand products. Some operations even established their own sweatshops or factory set-ups and workforces producing nothing but counterfeit products. In other quite extreme cases in the UK during 1993–94, it seemed that even when counterfeit traders were prosecuted they could avoid full prosecution and conviction under the Trades Description Act, by putting up signs stating that goods were indeed brand copies (see case study in section 5.3 under 'Trade Marks Act 1994').

To close a legal loophole, new anti-counterfeiting rules were introduced under criminal proceedings, as a remedy for counterfeit brand products. The updated rules for *statutory criminal offences* became effective from October 1994, introducing measures that allowed the agencies of trading standards and the police stronger powers to pursue immediate action towards 'career counterfeiters' and enabled the courts to seize assets of convicted counterfeiters.

The criminal mechanics now available for litigation are seen by many design and brand proprietors as a considerable improvement, compared to the more time-consuming actions brought through civil courts, criticised for being inadequate as a serious deterrent against infringements. The necessity for improved and stronger legislation in the field of counterfeit products is put into perspective when viewing the scale of counterfeit operations and their networks, together with the increasing value of goods confiscated in individual seizure operations carried out by the police and trading standards authorities. One single seizure which took place in the south-east of England in October 1996 resulted in the confiscation of luxury fashion brands worth £2 million.

Similar levels of organised counterfeiting appear throughout much of Continental Europe, with imitations of designer goods sold at markets and other impromptu stalls throughout cities. National sales of fashion counterfeits for a country such as Italy—reportedly the number one copying centre of Europe—are estimated to be in the range of £2.2 billion, with some individual seizure operations confiscating goods amounting to £4 million.

With the counterfeit trade existing not only on national levels but having expanded to operate internationally, suggestions being made from various agencies suggest that to fight the counterfeit operations with substantial impact, more wide-scale and Pan-European co-operation between national anti-counterfeit agencies and improved law structures are needed.

CASE STUDY

Silk supplier takes action

During the Première Vision exhibition in October 1993, a UK fabric supplier specialising in original silk designs sold six sample lengths of printed silk to a Belgian fashion company. No further orders for the print designs were placed by the fashion company, although subsequently garments carrying designs similar to three of the sample lengths supplied were discovered in the fashion company's outlets in Belgium, Paris, London and New York.

This discovery of very similar fabric, claimed by the silk supplier to infringe its copyright, led the UK company to take legal advice leading to civil proceedings in Belgium. When this case was published in the fashion trade press the silk supplier was taking legal advice regarding the possibility of bringing further action in the UK against the fashion company, which under UK law would be criminal rather than civil proceedings.

The case was finally won by the UK silk company, further details undisclosed.

When researching major UK textile trade exhibitions to establish how well companies producing original textile prints and designs were ensuring that samples clearly indicated to visitors any type of design/copyright ownership, unexpected discoveries were made. Taking into consideration that trade exhibitions often are the official showcases for textile companies to launch new and original designs, it was surprising to find that, if any, only around 5% of exhibitors display their claim of design right or copyright. Whereas details of cloth composition, reference number, weight and width appear clearly marked on all textile display hangers, no indication of the exhibitor's interest in copyright ownership was to be found on highly original designs.

Only in one instance was it possible to find a textile range clearly displaying all cloth designs with the information 'Copyright in the design of this fabric is the property of . . . (stating the name of the official copyright owner(s))'. By marking original designs with this clear indication of ownership right, a potential copier will think twice before producing illegal copies and the notification itself operates as an effective deterrent against counterfeiting. Another even simpler way of showing the copyright claim of an original and one-of-a-kind textile design would be to mark samples with the international copyright symbol © followed by the designer's (or the official owner's) name and year of first publication, e.g. © U.V. Nielsen, 1997.

Students and graduates, in particular, should take note and ensure their work is clearly marked with any copyright or other IP ownership claim when showing or exhibiting their original designs. At the same time for original designs which are to benefit from registered design protection, it is important to remember the requirement of the design not having been published or displayed prior to official registration unless specific permission is granted in advance by the Design Registry (see Chapter 3 'Premature disclosure' and 'Marking articles'). Other situations for designers and design students to avoid is leaving original designs with potential customers or sending original designs abroad. In these situations it is strongly recommended that *all* originals remain with the designers/creator at all times and only design copies are submitted if this is absolutely essential—again clearly marked with any copyright or other IP ownership claim of the original designs/collection.

In relation to showing original designs at trade exhibitions and the risk of being copied, it is worth noticing the growing support from some major European textile trade show organisers, for example Premiére Vision (PV). Following complaints from exhibitors that their textiles were being copied, the PV copyright unit 'Espace Copyright' was set up in 1995 to counteract fraud, copying and piracy on behalf of exhibitors. In cases of alleged copying the copyright unit will investigate, if necessary on an international level, to confirm the offence and track down the source of the copies. Also, during the four-day 'Premiére Vision' exhibition organisers are providing a free legal service to exhibitors and visitors, through a panel of specialist lawyers who can offer practical help to stop creations being copied. Should companies, however, find themselves too busy during the trade show to receive copyright information an appointment can be arranged free of charge with one of the Espace Copyright consultants represented in France, Germany, Italy, the Netherlands and the United Kingdom.

6.3 Primary and secondary infringement: producing, importing and reselling copies

Under the 1988 Act, liability does not merely apply to the person who initiates a copy or infringement. Liability also extends to those knowingly dealing in infringing articles, including reproduction of a design to produce exact or *substantially similar* articles, fraudulent use, application and any 'passing off' activities of a design. To prevent the continued infringe-ment, manufacture and sale of copies IP owners will often seek an injunc-tion followed by litigation for damages through the court system.

The level of damages awarded by the court depends on whether the infringement type is a 'primary' or 'secondary infringement': a manufac-turer or direct copier is a primary infringer while an importer, vendor, dealer or possessor of an infringing article for commercial purposes is a secondary infringer, who must be shown to have knowledge or reason to believe that the article is infringing before remedies can be granted.

If a secondary infringer is able to prove and maintain innocence, in most cases no damages can be obtained, although it may be possible to obtain an injunction. To remove this defence of innocence the plaintiff should, in the first instance, under qualified legal advice, put a notification to the infringer stating the claim of intellectual property before further action is taken.

Once the secondary infringer has been informed of the IP ownership claim, he or she will not be able to continue claiming innocence in the matter and must be seen to clearly co-operate to avoid further legal action such as injunctions or writs.

EXAMPLE

Primary or secondary infringements?

A company producing rainwear discovered that a major UK mail order company sold raincoats which clearly infringed the copyright of one of its own designs. Following legal advice to assess the situation, a writ was issued to the mail order company, not necessarily to pursue the company itself for infringement but with the main purpose of obtaining specific details of the supplier/manufacturer. Through the writ issued, the mail order organisation was in addition asked to state whether they approached *the manufacturer with a request for the raincoats to be produced or if* the garments were offered *to the company by the supplier/manufacturer. This particular information was required to establish if the mail order company was or had been involved in directing or procuring the copying to an extent that both parties—supplier and mail order company—were jointly or both severely liable for the alleged infringement. Alternatively, is could also be a case of the manufactur-er/supplier having full responsibility for the alleged copying (being the primary infringer) and the sales organisation (to the level of secondary infringement) having been unaware of dealing with an infringement product.*

6.4 Rights to seize infringing copies

According to the Copyright, Designs and Patents Act 1988 the IP proprietor can, under certain circumstances, seize and detain infringing goods
after giving official notice to the local police. Prior to any such seizure or
its preparation, *legal advice* should be sought on the matter.

The rights of seizure apply in particular instances where a street trader
or similar outlets do not have a permanent or regular place of business
and are selling infringing garments. Following the notice to local police
authorities, copies may then be seized provided that the copyright owner
does not enter any premises to which the public does not have access or
use any force. The design proprietor or the assigned representatives must
leave a prescribed notice giving information of the seizure.

On balance and although the law *does* allow the copyright owner the
right to personally seize goods as described above, it should also be considered that trading standards departments have a statutory duty to enforce
the Trade Descriptions Act as well as other duties under the copyright
law. The trading standards agencies, apart from carrying out their own
investigations and dealing with complaints from shoppers and other
traders, also follow up tip-offs and have powers to seize the goods of
counterfeit operations.

Current IP legislation also prohibits the import of counterfeit goods or
items believed to be infringements. It is therefore possible through the
Customs and Excise Commissioners to prevent the goods entering the
UK by notifying Customs to treat the goods as prohibited. The diffi-
culties in making use of this solution to halt counterfeit products at the
UK border are that one must be able to advise officials in advance, of the
date and place where the goods are likely to arrive in the UK. Also, the
copies may enter the United Kingdom through the initial borders of
other EU Member States and thereafter benefit from the free movement
regulations for goods operating within the European Union.

Returning to the British market, an example of one organisation which
actively works with police and trading standards authorities is the
Counterfeit Intelligence Bureau (CIB) in east London. Once the CIB
receives a complaint or tip-off, its workers join forces with the police to
gather evidence, obtain search warrants and seize goods which go
immediately into custody. Police will then question the counterfeiters and

CASE STUDY

Fashion label goes to court to recover its cloths

Police were called in by a London fashion company to investigate the loss of cloth worth £6,000 after a north London contract manufacturer failed to deliver 1000 garments of an order for more than 4,000 garments, destined for the high street and department stores.

The young fashion label had handed over the cloth after the CMT (cut/make/ trim) production order had been placed with the manufacturer. The accused claimed that the missing garments had not been made up properly and that the fashion company had given him permission to sell the garments to recover the cost of manufacturing and the cloth—a claim strongly denied by the fashion label.

In a separate bid to the police investigation, the fashion label also took High Court action to try and recover the missing cloth, garments made from it or damages . . . the company continues to try and recover the cloth.

---

bring charges under the Copyright, Designs and Patents Act 1988. The offence of infringement under the Criminal Justice Act carries *unlimited* fines and prison sentences of up to two years for company directors. In addition to the fines and damage claims, UK courts may also seize all assets which have arisen from serious and repetitive counterfeit operations, to disable the counterfeit operation starting up afresh in other locations.

6.5 Control of 'cabbage'—excess production

Within the fashion and clothing industries it is often found to be a popular belief that excess garments produced by sub-contractors cannot be controlled. However, excess production, also known in the trade as 'cabbage', is produced without the licence of the design owner by cutting surplus material from the design proprietor's production cutting pattern. Garments made in this way are the most exact form of copies possible and since they are made without a licence, their distribution can be restrained by infringement actions.

The following illustrates an extreme case where a design company was offered the opportunity to purchase its own copy merchandise from the 'cabbage' producer;

CASE STUDY

Designer wins 'cabbaging' case

A clothing and fabric design company won a case defending the right to its own fabric after a bizarre incident which saw the company being sold its own merchandise. The two-year case was centred on the 'cabbaging' of one of its outworkers.

The practice involves contracted manufacturers skimping on pattern layout to save fabric for themselves to sell on later. But the designer company only discovered it was the victim of such activity when the partner of one of its outworkers tried to sell waistcoats to the company's Sloane Street shop in London.

When the manager saw the waistcoats he was immediately suspicious, recognising the fabric to be an exclusive printed cotton velvet. He bought the waistcoats for £875 and took them to the company's headquarters where they were examined by directors and identified as being made of fabric supplied to outworkers one year previously.

The sales company belonging to the outworker's partner denied the allegations of cabbaging and took legal action over the non-payment of the invoice for the waistcoats. When challenged, the manufacturing company claimed the fabric was bought from a fabric supplier who later disproved the story.

In court, the judge found the 'cabbaging' allegations in favour of the design company, despite the fact that it was the same company which was being sued for non-payment. It was found that the fabric did belong to the design company all along. Costs estimated to be at least £5,000 was awarded to the clothing design company.

From the author's personal experience within different sectors of the clothing industry, it is, however, also clear that for a number of cases the 'cabbage' production is distributed in such small quantities, that there is not enough commercial justification in seeking to stop or control the infringement using the machinery of law, although this is possible. Instead, the intellectual property owner should ensure written terms and conditions via contracts with the sub-contractor, whereby they specifically agree they are not permitted to manufacture garments to a particular design other than for the owner of that design. The sub-contractor should sign a copy of the terms and conditions to indicate its acceptance.

The contractual agreement must aim to cover all possible trading options between the 'sub-contractor' and 'buyer' (design company).

Typically this will involve the specification of copyright ownership and reliability in the following business situations:

- *When goods are manufactured/supplied to the buyer's design.* The supplier should acknowledge that copyright and all other intellectual property rights are vested in and belong to the 'buyer' throughout the world. The supplier will have and acquire no IP rights through its work.
- *When goods purchased from the supplier have not been designed by the buying company.* The supplier must warrant that the product—in part and/or completeness—does not infringe any intellectual property rights or regulations in the United Kingdom, European Community or any other country - including the country of origin.
- Should the 'buyer' at any stage suffer any liability of infringement or counterfeit claims under current or new legislation, be it for design, copyright, registered design, trade mark or other IP rights, the supplier will, through the contract, be bound to compensate the buyer for resulting losses and damages.
- *Confidentiality.* The supplier must treat designs and other intellectual property in the strictest confidence and not disclose, copy or reproduce any work in part or complete form. This must include all documents, designs, know-how, patterns, trade mark/brand name material and all information supplied from the 'buyer' in connection to the work, which at any given time must be treated as confidential, i.e. not be made publicly available. All of the afore-mentioned items must be acknowledged by the contractor to remain the property of the 'buyer' throughout the contract and hence kept safe and returned in good condition to the buyer together with any copies, notes and excess items once the contract is completed or at any time on demand.
- *Excess production and 'seconds' with faults.* Precise instructions must exist for the clearance/distribution of any excess or faulty garment/textile pieces arising from samples and the bulk production. The 'buyer' may wish to accept delivery of *all* overrun units and faulty items to maintain full control over the distribution of a design or trade mark. Alternatively, certain levels of excess production may be accepted as part of the order (e.g. +/- 10% of the contract quantity). Often the sub-contractor will be allowed to sell the faulty and/or excess goods through agents at clearance prices. However, such clearance sales should only be allowed under the obligation that the manufacturer is responsible for the complete removal of *all* trade mark labelling, trimmings and packaging materials which refer to the intellectual property owner. It will also be a good idea to specify the exact sources, e.g. geographic areas where samples, faulty items and excess clothing may be sold (refer to the following case study).

The contractual intellectual property elements described above are only a few examples of the fields to be covered through written agreements when working with sub-contractors. In all cases it is important that contracts are drawn up under professional assistance preferably by a legal specialist—as opposed to any 'do-it-yourself' contract versions—to ensure that the document is legally correct and meets the needs of the individual company in the trading environment.

When working with overseas companies involved in fabric and clothing production, the necessity of written terms and acknowledged obligations becomes even more important in the process of protecting designs against infringement or misuse through sub-contractors, import agents, other businesses and individuals. Do not assume that local legislation automatically provides the same level of business standards and automatic protection rights as in the United Kingdom—it may or may not be the case. Even where national legislation appears to be sufficient, it would still be advisable to include intellectual property rights in the contract format to ensure that the overseas supplier clearly understands his obligations fully to protect the intellectual property in any format, be it components or complete garments. An example of how excess and faulty production pieces can result in infringement on a considerable scale is shown in the following case study.

CASE STUDY

Infringement through clearance sales (1996)

An up-market menswear brand trading through its own retail outlets and several independent stockists throughout the UK, established in the mid-1990s a very strong trade mark with tremendous brand recognition, with particular strength of the special-dyed innovative fabrics developed for the brand and the advanced product branding, using several special labels on each design to reinforce the trade mark image and design value.

Portugal had proved to be a particularly good source for developing new fabrics and with very short lead times allowing quick-response production for fashion-led products. For several seasons Portuguese factories supplied a growing number of garments manufactured to the menswear company's design specifications, then suddenly a considerable number of the branded garments with minor faults started to appear in the UK through discount retailers, many with all original trade mark labels still attached.

The availability of branded garments retailing through discount outlets at merely 20% of the recommended retail price with only minor faults, caused grave concern both for the trade mark owner and the appointed UK import company as neither had authorised sales of reject garments to any UK outlet. The general understanding between the buyer and sub-contractors, was for the Portuguese factories only to sell small quantities of samples, excess production or faulty garments through local markets and only when all traces of the trade mark had been fully removed from the garments.

Following investigations, it was found that as the trade mark popularity and overall sales grew, orders increased from small trial productions of 400 units to orders for 10000 units, although the reject rate remained around 5%. In reality the factory instead of clearing only 20 faulty garments now had to dispose of 500 units. While local markets could absorb small quantities, 500 faulty units were too many. The factory therefore made an independent decision to sell all rejects in one major lot to a larger clearing agent based in Ireland, unaware that the Irish agent's usual sales channels included selling goods on to various discount retailers in the United Kingdom, resulting in the uncontrolled influx of reject garments selling at discount prices within the same geographical area as the full-price branded clothing range sold by the trade mark owner.

It may be argued that the manufacturer in this case failed to meet the obligations of trade mark removal prior to clearance and should have consulted the trade mark owner prior to a major clearance sale. However, it is also possible that written agreements did not emphasise the issue sufficiently to cause concern for the overseas manufacturer. To eliminate the problem of losing control over future excess production or reject garments, the trade mark owner established a special agreement with sub-contractors whereby all clearance garments would be bought at a special rate, giving the trade mark owner full control over clearance operations.

6.6 Legal advice

In the day-to-day running of a business, the expertise of lawyers specialising in intellectual property is seen by many clothing companies as an unnecessary expense. Often companies will wait until they suddenly receive a writ or solicitor's letter before seeking legal advice. At the same time, some companies develop their own DIY versions of legal documents and contracts, without realising the complexity of various legal issues and how binding they are. Some lawyers specialising in the fashion industry have consistently found that many companies and designers draft and sign legal documents for intellectual property without thorough advice from legal experts. As a result the documents use terms and conditions which are more damaging than helpful, and legally place the company or individual in a very difficult position.

It is important to stress that apart from just reacting to litigious claims, solicitors can help ensure that all documents and contracts are legally 'watertight', that designs are adequately protected and, where possible, lawsuits are avoided.

Consulting a lawyer from the start and on a regular basis, involving him/her in normal business activities will help the solicitor gain a fuller understanding of the specific company, its background and future projections. So when a problem does arise, the solicitor will be better equipped to understand how the problem arose and how to legally deal with it. By taking qualified and professional legal advice first, the company will ideally be able to avoid being locked into situations of litigation altogether.

When seeking legal advice in the field of intellectual property rights and legislation, companies should be aware that not all lawyers have the same skills. As in most other industries, different lawyers have different areas of expertise. Apart from the fact that legislation and legal matters in general are complex subjects, the wide span of law means that lawyers naturally specialise in particular fields be they civil or commercial law, taxation, property or other legislative fields.

It is therefore important to take legal assistance from solicitors who are familiar with specific industry needs such as clothing and textiles and who have sound experience in the related law. In recognising the increasing demand from businesses for advice on intellectual property legislation a growing number of law firms have established departments specialising in IP law and rights.

Also, an increasing number of independent organisations in the UK focus on protection of design and other intellectual property. The aim is to keep members informed and up to date on legal developments, law changes and sometimes also to offer facilities of qualified legal advice in potential infringement cases.

6.7 Independent copyright organisations in the UK

With designers' and managers' growing concern for protecting intellectual property sufficiently, recent years have seen the creation of several independent organisations working predominantly with intellectual property rights. The main purpose of such copyright organisations is to keep members informed of IP legislation, new developments, how to protect intellectual property in practical terms and generally uphold the rights and interests of original design owners.

Several organisations can offer full-time access to legal advice in connection with possible infringement issues, assist with solving business disputes or provide specialist witnesses during litigation. Also the available litigation insurance policies should be considered, to reduce the financial strain of taking legal action to protect intellectual property rights.

Other member facilities include structures to log work protected by automatic design right and copyright, thereby strengthening the claim for automatic rights, which by law do not require official registration and, as a result, can be more difficult to prove in infringement cases. However, if in-house records contain the necessary details to prove ownership of design it may be less useful to join an organisation that mainly logs automatically protected copyright work but does not offer legal advice which may be more important to the individual business. It is therefore recommended that individual designers and companies assess the different facilities offered by the various independent organisations to clearly determine the benefits and usefulness of membership to their business. Some copyright organisations may cater for particular industries or types of intellectual property, so make sure to research and weigh up the options before making the commitment to join a copyright protection organisation.

In general, by joining a copyright organisation members may, in some cases, be able to benefit from using the organisation's logo for business letterheads, swing tickets and advertisements, as well as display material for showrooms and exhibitions, clearly promoting a design company's interest in protecting its intellectual property rights and acting as a deterrent.

 One organisation well-known to many fashion companies is the 'Fashion Design Protection Associates' (FDPA) founded in 1974. Its purpose to 'uphold the rights of originators of creative fashion designs'. The services offered through FDPA membership include:

- confidential consultancy services to help prevent infringements and suggest the steps to be taken to stop counterfeiting;
- provision of expert witnesses for the purpose of court evidence;
- systems to assist members in establishing copyright/design right in fashion designs;
- an arbitration service in disputes concerning copying and design rights;
- legal fees insurance.

The organisation will explore every avenue to settle disputes without litigation as well as acting as a vetting agency for members to ensure that companies do not go into expensive litigation unless they have a strong chance of succeeding. Further objectives of this organisation include working to support appropriate changes in the law relating to intellectual property protection and the interests of members, as well as supporting a high moral attitude in the trade towards original designs and the manufacturing of such clothing/textile articles.

For details of intellectual property associations see Address List including:

- Fashion Design Protection Associates (FDPA);
- Design and Artists Copyright Society (DACS);
- Chartered Society of Designers (CSD);
- British Copyright Council;
- Anti Copying In Design (ACID).

Legal fees insurance

In the field of insurance a limited number of insurance brokers offer certain policies which greatly reduce the financial impact of legal fees in cases of litigation. However, the area of legal fees insurance is viewed as high risk by the majority of insurance companies which can result in very high premiums from high street insurers. It is therefore not surprising that some intellectual property organisations in recent years have started to negotiate specialised insurance policies on behalf of their members.

As an example of one policy structure and to allow better insight into the advantages linked to this type of litigation insurance a brief outline follows of the legal fees insurance available through the Fashion Design Protection Associates for copyright and design right enforcement.

The insurance has been established specifically for FDPA members and, as such, the organisation is requested, in cases of copyright dispute, to work as a vetting agency to fully explore the case and make every effort to settle it, supported by the fact that if the infringer refuses to reach a mutual settlement the FDPA member has the legal fees insurance of £100,000 for up to 90% of legal costs and expenses, to pursue the infringement through litigation.[4]

By exploring each individual case, the copyright organisation also investigates the infringer's financial status to ensure he is of sufficient financial standing to pay at least twice the estimated legal costs and expenses. This financial consideration again highlights the necessity in any copyright case to evaluate and balance the advantages and risk factors of legal action, thereby addressing the question whether action is likely to be able to both stop the infringement *and* recover lost profits suffered from the copying or whether the main result of any action will be limited to stopping the production and sales of infringing goods, without the likelihood of recovering legal expenses and loss of profit.

If the initial negotiations with the copying party do fail and on close examination it is felt upon FDPA assessment that the case is very likely to be won, the next step for the FDPA liaison officer will be to appoint a solicitor to give a legal opinion on the chances of success and to estimate the costs. The solicitor's fee, currently fixed at £1,000, will be paid 50% by the insurance company and 50% by the insured.

Thereafter, if the prospects of successful litigation in the solicitor's legal opinion is 70% or more, subsequent legal fees are covered through the policy ranging between 75–90% of all costs depending on the individual turnover of the business. On a sliding scale smaller companies with a turnover of up to £1.5 million will generally receive 90% of legal costs, while businesses with an annual turnover ranging between £5–20 million will achieve up to 75% of the legal costs through the insurance scheme.

One requirement for the design company to maintain throughout the duration of its FDPA insurance policy is to post a sealed envelope of design photocopies—signed and dated—of all original styles to be insured to the independent registry IPPR (the Intellectual Property Policy Registry). Once received, the Registry will log all the designs and issue an official receipt. The charges for registering these designs are included in the insurance premium and there is no limit to the number of designs which the policyholder can register.

The yearly cost involved for this particular legal fees policy is £1 per £1,000 of turnover, with reductions for large turnovers and a minimum yearly premium of £500. The overall limit of indemnity available is £100,000 in one year, while policyholders, after a no claims period of one year—similar to standard insurance policies—qualify for a 'no claims' bonus of 20% upon policy renewal.

The advantage of such insurance policies as described here is that no longer do small companies producing original designs have to remain passive when discovering that their original design articles are being copied because they find the legal costs prohibitive. This means that small design companies can avoid a situation whereby they find themselves forced not to enforce their legal rights because 'the infringer drags on the litigation until they run out of funds'.[4] In many cases the financial muscle available through the insurance policy can often function as a copying deterrent and be a strong bargaining tool in negotiating a settlement, without going into full litigation. Also, insurance policies whereby the copyright protection organisation examines all options and vets the case thoroughly before litigation, means that very high levels of successful litigation are achieved. In the case of the FDPA legal fees insurance, this has, over a two-year period, produced a 99% rate of success with all client cases.[4]

Insurance policies are available through different insurance companies and copyright organisations, not only for automatic intellectual property categories—copyright and design right—but include litigation policies for registered design, trade marks and patents. A certain amount of research may be required by the individual clothing/textile company to achieve the most competitive quote and advantageous policy. For insurance purposes it is worthwhile considering that officially registered intellectual property, such as registered design, trade marks and patents are generally cheaper to insure, compared to unregistered IP works.

It is a good idea to contact specialist copyright organisations who will either have insurance policies available through membership or alternatively will be able to advise of specialist insurance brokers for the fashion industry.

6.8 Clothing companies addressing counterfeiting

As designs and trade marks are viewed by more and more companies as important business assets, many corporate strategies have developed in the 1990s making it highly visible to competitors and any possible counterfeiters that misuse of a company's intellectual property, be it original designs or trade marks, will not be tolerated.

Several preventive measures are also used by companies, one example detailed earlier in the book includes the measures operated by the registered trade mark Lycra® (refer to Chapter 5 section 5.3, 'Registered trade marks for the fashion industry'). For instance, should a retailer or manufacturer suspect that a garment or fabric wrongly claims to contain the branded Lycra fibre, the trade mark proprietor offers to test the material free of charge, which is clearly in the interests of both the retailer and trade mark owner. This simple assurance/testing policy greatly assists in the elimination of brand imitations being promoted as the original quality fibre, apart from the problem of imitation fibres being promoted as 'Lycra', thereby deceiving the customer who thinks she is buying the quality brand. During wash and wear, the garment will soon lack the performance standards of a true Lycra® elastane garment, and consumers be dissatisfied by what they wrongly believe to be a branded quality fibre/garment.

Another example of strong brand protection policy from the clothing industry is found in the jeans wear industry. A company such as **Levi Strauss**, leaves no doubt as to the legal action it is prepared to take against counterfeiters in order to protect the Levi's trade mark, making its stand through large advert warnings in trade journals, e.g. *Drapers Record*, *Fashion Weekly*, *Menswear* and *Marketer & Discount Trader*. One such advert showed a pair of handcuffs accompanied by the text 'Sell a fake pair of our jeans and you could end up wearing *them*' or in cases where second-hand jeans have been over-dyed 'Refinish our jeans and you could end up wearing *a pair*' (in both instances the text is referring to the illustrated handcuffs). Another advert/warning for potential counterfeiters brings attention to and illustrates the penalties which can be expected if copying their jeans wear brand and products, reading 'Rip off our label and you might end up with one of your own' referring to the advert's photograph of a prosecuted wholesaler, sentenced to six months in prison (shown by the use of an actor) (see Figures 6.1 and 6.2).

In addition to IP proprietors marking the individual design/garment with copyright symbols or design right wording, patent or trade mark registration number, companies can also publicise their rights and property claims in the trade press to warn off counterfeit operations.

Conversely, a business which is found to infringe intellectual owner-ship rights may be forced—as part of the dispute settlement— to make a substantial public statement to 'admit' its infringements. For example:

> 'Euro High' Ltd (proxy name) apologise to 'Many Stores' Ltd (proxy name), for any confusion which may have been caused as a result of use by us of a logo closely resem-bling the 'Many Stores' logo, which is a registered trade mark of 'Many Stores' Ltd.

Figure 6.1 Levi Strauss counterfeit warning—legal action. Reproduced with the permission of Levi Strauss (UK) Press Office © Levi Strauss September 1990

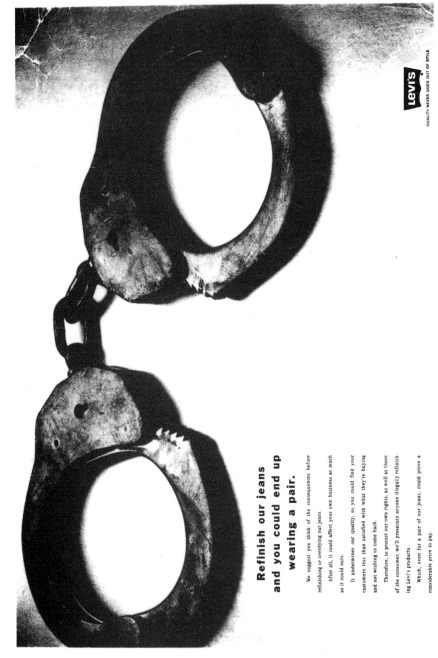

**Refinish our jeans
and you could end up
wearing a pair.**

We suggest you think of the consequences before
refinishing or overdying our jeans.

After all, it could affect your own business as much
as it could ours.

It undermines our quality, so you could find your
customers less than satisfied with what they're buying
and not wishing to come back.

Therefore, to protect our own rights, as well as those
of the consumer, we'll prosecute anyone illegally refinishing Levi's products.

Which, even for a pair of our jeans, could prove a
considerable price to pay.

LEVI'S
QUALITY NEVER GOES OUT OF STYLE

Figure 6.2 Levi Strauss counterfeit warning—prosecution. Reproduced with the permission of Levi Strauss (UK) Press Office © Levi Strauss March 1992

EXAMPLE

Intellectual property rights announced in trade journal

Legal action on copyright and 'passing off' by 'HIGHNESS' Ltd (proxy name)
. . . To date, action has been brought and interlocutory orders have successfully been obtained against those involved with garments bearing the 'Highness' name or its well known designs and logos or names so similar as to be misleading.
. . . The 'Highness' company has obtained a number of High Court injunctions and has successfully obtained and executed search and seize orders enabling its representatives to enter premises all over the United Kingdom and Europe where counterfeit garments have been found being manufactured for sale and seizing those illegal garments.
. . . Highness Ltd retains ownership of all rights in its designs and name. Genuine 'Highness' garments can only be purchased from 'Highness' outlets. Similar garments offered for sale elsewhere will inevitably be cheap unauthorised copies and 'Highness Ltd' will not hesitate to take legal action against anyone who it discovers to be dealing in such goods, whether or not this is the manufacturer, wholesaler or retailer. . . .

6.9 Company case study: *Monsoon*

Since the launch of the Monsoon women's wear brand a substantial competitive edge has developed from the company's range of high quality, distinctive and original prints available exclusively under the Monsoon trade mark. However, the company also discovered that in the UK high street a growing number of multiple retailers were starting to copy and directly infringe the original textile designs of Monsoon. To combat the growing problem the fashion brand initiated, between 1989–94, a legal blitz against firms counterfeiting its designs, in order to protect the textile and garment designs which were being sold in the UK through more than 65 branches.

One of the most powerful infringement actions taken by the company took place in July 1993, when Monsoon successfully brought a copyright action based on criminal law against a large UK discount chain with 150 fashion stores. The difference of the court recognising action according to criminal law, meant that the case was resolved in *weeks* rather than years and the costs were therefore considerably less, compared to a case under civil law.

CASE STUDY

Monsoon vs. multiple discount chain

Following the discovery by a Monsoon employee that a discount chain was selling identical copies of Monsoon's printed skirts, the retail chain was issued with design right writs by Monsoon.

The criminal prosecution proved the infringer was knowingly selling copies, and the discount chain was by Court Order forced to remove from sale and hand over 1100 infringing copy garments which had been produced and supplied to the discount chain from India and other Far East countries.

Furthermore the discount stores had to pay £10,000 in legal costs, plus a five figure settlement to avoid further legal action by Monsoon lawyers.

Identical copy of an original textile design: © Monsoon Ltd, UK.

Photographic material reproduced with the permission of Solo Syndication Ltd

The legal costs for Monsoon in this case amounted to £8,000 (costs which the infringing company was ordered to pay). The difference in cost and time by suing according to UK criminal law, often means the dispute can be solved in a matter of weeks, compared to civil law action which can take substantially longer. This can be illustrated by another Monsoon copyright case against a well-known high street retail chain selling fashion garments to teenagers throughout the UK.

Cost and time factors of legal civil action

*To protect copyright of original designs in this incidence the legal case was brought under a civil action, against a multiple retail chain involving a number of Monsoon garment designs, took **four years** to solve and amounted to legal costs of more than £20,000.*

The case involved three Monsoon designs which had found their way into the multiple retail chain. After threats to issue proceedings from Monsoon's lawyers the retailer agreed not to sell garments which infringed Monsoon's copyright.

Despite that agreement, Monsoon found that the retail chain was continuing to sell infringing garments and it was decided that action through the courts was necessary. During the four-year legal dispute the retail chain did in fact admit that 679 garments were sold after the agreement to stop sales of infringing designs.

The final outcome was for the infringing retail chain to accept a High Court settlement whereby it paid a five-figure settlement, legal costs plus an undisclosed sum to Monsoon for damages, after admitting infringing the copyright of all three designs.

Reproduced by permission of Monsoon Ltd (UK)/© Monsoon Ltd, 1993

The option of criminal procedure was made possible after the introduction of the 1988 Copyright, Designs and Patents Act, making it a criminal offence to make, import, distribute and/or sell infringing copies knowingly (to ensure an alleged infringer cannot claim to be innocent of knowingly dealing with counterfeit articles refer to earlier chapters dealing with 'Marking articles' and Chapter 6 'Primary and secondary infringement'). The criminal action brought by Monsoon and described in the case study on the following pages, marked the first time a fashion house used this novel remedy against someone handling garments which they knew were infringements.

It should be highlighted that bringing action under criminal law is only used in 'watertight' cases supported by strong legal evidence. However, the infringer, if prosecuted successfully, faces unlimited fines and court costs and the directors risk jail sentences of up to two years' imprisonment.

On this basis companies should realise that infringement is not worth the risk. Original fashion/design companies such as Monsoon reinforce this warning: 'If you steal our designs we will injunction your importers, put your distributors in the dock and summon every shop and street trader we find'. Potential infringers should also consider that 'for the cost of the court case and fine, a company could buy hundreds of original works from textile designers, it would be giving them work, it would make the purchaser profitable and they would have an original end product' (Peter Simon, Chairman of Monsoon, © 1993, Monsoon press release).

6.10 Public perception of counterfeit goods

In the process of protecting designs and trade marks against infringements one factor which has come to be viewed by many intellectual property owners as an increasingly important element is the consumers' attitude towards counterfeiting and brand copies.

A large proportion of consumers express a worrying attitude towards counterfeit products whereby the purchase of copies is merely seen morally as being 'slightly naughty' with the attraction of severely low prices of the brand imitation being too big a factor to resist buying the imitation goods. Also, any obvious disadvantages linked to copies are often disregarded by the consumer, e.g. being left without any guarantee or the option of returning or exchanging faulty goods. On a larger economic scale the effects include the loss of tax revenue for the state and the trade mark owner's loss of sale and market share followed by the knock-on effect of the company's profitability and ability to maintain employment levels for its workforce. At the same time it seems that shoppers tend to ignore the moral issue, that any money they *do* part with when buying a copy product, often helps to maintain illegal, low-paid workforces while those responsible for running counterfeit operations use profits to be invested in more criminal operations.

One way for intellectual property owners to try and stop the large-scale counterfeit systems has been to launch national anti-copying agencies or departments, which, in co-operation with official authorities and the police, weed out illegal production and trade. However, when defending intellectual property rights internationally—even within European countries—the level of success in trying to stop counterfeiters will often depend on the legislation at each national level. Whereas the United Kingdom now has legislation which allows police forces much more effective action, the same may not be the case in other EU countries.

Representing Italian prestige brand owners fighting against imitation products, the organisation Indicam highlighted the national legislation aspect in 1995: 'Potential investors may be keen on Italy because it has the expertise and the raw materials. But if they weigh up the risks of rip-offs of their products, they may well decide to go to a country where their product is better protected' (*The Times*, 1995).

6.11 Customer and stockist education/ information: new approach to dealing with counterfeits

In the United Kingdom several companies have, in recent years, started to include new strategies of consumer and retail education/information programmes as one of several important remedies to help beat counterfeit products.

An example of this approach has been initiated by the high quality outdoor clothing and shoe label 'Timberland'. In cooperation with Trading Standards Officers the company launched, in December 1994, a campaign to educate consumers about the damage caused to retailers and the economy by counterfeiting. The information programme included radio interviews which were broadcast by several stations across the UK, to make consumers realise the effect of counterfeit products.

As expressed by the Timberland brand marketing manager: '*Most people who buy fakes are unaware of the effect that the counterfeit industry has, for example on unemployment . . . If counterfeiters sell fake branded products . . . this means that jobs will be lost, not only at retail but also within the company which owns the target brand and within those companies which supply components*' (*Drapers Record*, 1994).

In addition to radio broadcasting, the initial campaign also included information packs being sent to 'Timberland' stockists and setting up a customer hotline available to both stockists and consumers when encountering counterfeit goods. The next step in the anti-copying campaign was planning to involve linking up with other brands to launch joint publicity campaigns highlighting the impact of IP infringements.

Similar brand protection campaigns by other fashion companies with branded product ranges include creating much closer business links and obligations with stockists. This may involve the agreement of retail buyers to operate as 'brand protectors', not only in the interests of the IP owner but also to ensure the retailer at local level remains vigilant towards unfair competition or outlets passing off imitation products to consumers.

Anti-copying campaigns by well-known brand names within the textile and clothing sectors include addressing consumers directly, through the national press and media, to discourage them from buying counterfeit garments and articles. This approach aims to effectively eradicate any consumer demand which may exist for cheap, poor quality and illegal counterfeit products. An example of the direct customer information strategy is illustrated opposite.

6.12 Summary

As described in this chapter several types of action can be taken by the design and/or trade mark owner to stop the illegal activities of counterfeiting and passing off. Predominantly, prevention will be better than cure, for example by drawing up contracts with all suppliers and various sub-contractors—both within the UK and overseas—that clearly state the terms and IP obligations under which business is to be carried out between the intellectual property owner and any supplier/manufacturer. In the case of competitors selling infringing designs, a considerable range of copyright organisations, lawyers specialising in IP legislation and trading standards departments will be able to advise on the action to be taken and to assess whether to pursue legal action.

A decisive factor in pursuing legal action in infringement cases is still the potential level of costs involved. This can leave individual designers and smaller companies producing original designs prisoners of legal fees when instigated by financially stronger but less innovative competitors. For this reason membership of copyright protection organisations and

BY APPOINTMENT TO
H.R.H. THE PRINCE OF WALES
OUTFITTERS J & J CROMBIE LTD LEEDS

CROMBIE

CROMBIE® IS NOT AN ORDINARY WORD

CROMBIE® is the Registered Trade Mark of **J & J CROMBIE Limited** who for over 190 years have applied this mark to distinguish a wide variety of high quality cloths and clothing. The Trade Mark CROMBIE® has been used since 1805 for the sale of cloth, clothing and the legendary CROMBIE® coat. **J & J CROMBIE Limited's** reputation for manufacturing high quality cloth and clothing is such that the CROMBIE® Trade Mark has acquired a world-wide reputation second to none

Only genuine CROMBIE® cloth and clothing can bear the CROMBIE® Trade Mark

Be warned that unscrupulous traders sometimes use illegal expressions such as CROMBIE® style, CROMBIE® look, CROMBIE® type or imitation CROMBIE® to describe their inferior cloths and clothing in an attempt to deliberately and fraudulently mislead

Traders contemplating such acts should take note that **J & J CROMBIE Limited** will without exception take all steps necessary to stop this illegal misuse of their valuable Trade Name and protect the public

CROMBIE® by CROMBIE®

The cloth that became the coat that became the legend

J & J Crombie Limited Glenesk Mills Langholm DG13 0LA (01274) 542255
A member of the Illingworth, Morris Group of Companies

Figure 6.3 Crombie advertisement published in the UK press. Reproduced with the permission of J&J Crombie Ltd © 1996 Illingworth Morris Ltd

legal insurance to cover litigation fees can prove crucial. Other long-term benefits in taking up membership with a copyright protection association include being able to keep up to date with legislative developments, having access to organisations' confidential consultancy services and/or specialist legal advisers, provision of expert witnesses for legal evidence and the use of the copyright organisation's logo on business and promotional material as a deterrent against possible counterfeiters.

In the event of discovering potential infringements of designs or trade marks certain preliminary and practical measures should be taken to assess if, in accordance with current legislation, there is a case of infringement to be defended. The preliminary measures which should be taken include, if possible, the purhase of at least one of the offending garments/articles. Then, the matter must be placed immediately before legal advisers for a balanced assessment of the legal strengths, weaknesses and risk factors of the alleged infringement.

If a decision is made to proceed with further action to stop the production and sale of copies, it is important to explore and make every effort to settle the dispute with the support of legal advisers. Should all efforts fail to solve the matter at this stage further remedies against counterfeiting include:

- *Interlocutory injunction*—to halt the production and sale of imitation products.
- *Obtaining evidence via a court order*—used in cases to force the co-operation of an alleged infringer.
- *'Anton Piller' court order*—used in exceptional instances to allow the plaintiff or the legal advisers to search and access the defendant's premises including stock, documents and other valuable evidence.
- *Counterfeit seizure*—the right of seizure can be used in particular instances where a street trader or similar outlet of copies does not have a permanent or regular place of business. Advance notification must be made to the local police authorities.
- *Court action under civil or criminal law*—depending on the type of evidence, level of illegal and/or criminal offence by the infringing party and according to how 'watertight' allegations are, legal action can be taken under civil or criminal law. In general, civil action tends to take longer and be more costly, compared to criminal action where cases may be settled within weeks and carry heavy fines and possible jail sentences for convicted defendants.
- *Final injunction*—following a successful court action a final restraining order will usually be issued by the court to prevent the defending party from producing any further copies or committing any other acts of infringement. Also, decisions will be made regarding the infringing goods/materials, e.g. to be destroyed or handed over to the plaintiff.

- *Monetary claims*—the court will decide, based on calculations, the level of damages to be awarded to the plaintiff following successful action. The underlying principle is that the intellectual property owner should at least be no worse off had the infringement not taken place.

While all of the above remedies are available to take action against various infringements, prevention rather than cure is strongly recommended. As illustrated by the business strategies and campaigns developing from many well-known fashion companies, by clearly showing that a company or individual designer takes its intellectual property rights seriously and will not tolerate copying a deterrent factor is created for possible infringers to think twice. At the same time educating and informing consumers of the financial effects of supporting ill-produced copies will, in the long term, hopefully eliminate any demand for cheap counterfeit articles.

7

DESIGN PROTECTION IN THE EUROPEAN SINGLE MARKET

7.1 International protection of intellectual property

Currently no all-embracing international registration and protection system exists for intellectual property forms such as copyright, patent, registered design or trade marks. Although systems are available across national borders for protection categories such as patents and more recently European trade marks, *one* international system does not exist whereby a single application achieves the IP ownership and protection rights which truly constitute 'worldwide' ownership rights. Instead, the ownership and protection rights granted under any international system will be limited to the countries which are signatory members of that particular agreement/international protection system.

However, when a designer or company wishes to protect intellectual property outside its own country it is worth being fully aware of and up to date with agreements made between countries which provide special advantages to already registered intellectual property from the United Kingdom or other nations. As an example, for the United Kingdom certain countries extend protection to include UK registered designs. These states are mainly members of the Commonwealth which have enacted local legislation whereby having completed certain local formalities the UK registration is accepted as being equivalent to an independent registration in the country concerned (a list of these countries is found in Chapter 5 section 5.2 'Priority dates').

Other international conventions such as the Berne Convention, only state that signatory countries must not discriminate against overseas applicants and member states are only obliged to provide the same level of protection as granted to a country's own nationals, disregarding whether this is weaker or stronger than protection available under UK legislation.

International conventions do, however, allow for the use of 'priority claims' whereby applicants from membership countries, within 6–12 months of the initial application (depending on the individual agreement), can file the necessary documents in other convention signatory countries claiming the official date to be that of the very first application filed. However, in most cases the applicant still has to fill in local documents complying with the legal requirements of the individual country concerned, as well as paying the necessary fees.

A company considering protection abroad should, as a result, try to evaluate the potential market in a foreign country and the cost as well as time involved in obtaining design protection. It may be that the resources required will not justify obtaining protection, although the design obviously will then be freely available for exploitation by others.[11]

7.2 Legislation and development stages of European and international IP protection

When looking at intellectual property legislation available on a European and international level for the main categories of IP protection—patents, industrial design and trade mark legislation—very different levels of developmental progress and actual legislation exist.

Patents

Since 1977 the European Patent Office (EPO) has existed to allow registrations of European patents, following similar application, search and registration procedures as used in the United Kingdom. On an international scale, the 'Patent Co-operation Treaty' (PCT) came into force in 1978 providing the closest possible equivalent to a worldwide system for simplified filing of a patent application (valid within the PCT signatory countries of around 90 member states).

Trade mark registration

Only comparatively recently, since January 1996, has it been possible to apply for a Community (European Community) trade mark through the EU office based in Alicante, Spain.

In addition to the EU Community trade mark another new international trade mark system has been provided under the well-established Madrid Protocol (enforced April 1, 1996), but as only 12 countries have signed this particular agreement—six of these belonging to the EU—in effect it will still be some time before the international trade mark system achieves any real international effect. Therefore outside the European Union, brand name rights continue to be dealt with on a national level.

Industrial design protection

Due to the very diverse nature of national legislation within the European Community, negotiations to develop European design legislation have involved several lengthy stages of discussions leading towards each country starting to introduce national legislation changes to accommodate new European law. From the Green Paper published in 1991 the legislation proposal moved on in January 1994 to the stage of a regulation for Community design protection, *at the time of writing still subject to ongoing regulation amendments produced in March 1997 and the final approval by EU Member States*. Provided that EU countries implement the necessary national legislation changes to accommodate new European design law (as requested by the amended EU Directive to be in place by EU Member States on January 1, 1998), it is hoped that Community design legislation and the EU design protection will be a reality before the year 2000.

Considering that many fast-moving fashion industries are likely to achieve the greatest short-term benefits from Community trade marks— and hopefully, in the near future, Community design protection—the following section will only include very brief reference to some of the overall benefits arising from the European patent system, mainly for the purpose of indicating advantages still to develop for other protection categories more applicable for fashion businesses and their design protection.

The following will be an outline of the recently established Community trade mark system, particularly apt for the large part of fashion companies where image and market reputation often build on trade mark recognition, hence the importance of protecting brand names sufficiently both in the UK and European export market.

By examining the main features of the Community design regulations—although actual legislation has not come into force as yet—the reader will have the opportunity to consider and anticipate developments and the legislation likely to be introduced in the near future for design protection on a European scale.

7.3 European patents

The European Patent Office (EPO) is a result of intergovernmental co-operation and negotiations resulting in the European Patent Convention, which came into force in 1977. However, the EPO is not an EU institution but is a completely self-financing organisation with its head office in Munich (sub-offices in The Hague, Berlin and Vienna) using unitary and centralised procedures to grant Europeans patents.

The three main criteria for patentability are: novelty, inventive step and industrial applicability. By filing a single patent application (in French, German or English language) following successful examination and search procedures, it is possible to obtain patent protection in all 17 member states of the organisation valid for up to 20 years. As a guideline a European patent normally costs less than three separate national patents and can be filed either with a national patent office or directly to the EPO.

Member states include—both EU countries and some EFTA states—the following: Austria, Belgium, Denmark, France, Germany, Greece, Ireland, Italy, Liechtenstein, Luxembourg, Monaco, the Netherlands, Portugal, Spain, Sweden, Switzerland and the United Kingdom. (Further European countries are expected to join in due course.)

Once the patent is granted, rights are transferred to the countries designated by the applicant in the initial application, where the same level of legal protection is achieved as for national patents. Similar to the UK patent system patents are granted following an in–depth examination and comprehensive novelty search (based on a collection of over 28 million documents) and once the exclusive patent rights are established the technical information is available to the public through databases and patent libraries.

Through the use of new information technology, with the specific aim of providing services to the European industry, individuals and small companies, the EPO is becoming much more accessible both for general communication and specific patent information search to the public via CD-ROM systems and Internet connection. The EPO information pages on the Internet—including latest news, press releases, EPO publications and lists of frequently asked questions (FAQs)—are found at the location: http://www.epo.co.at/epo/.

7.4 Community trade marks

Since January 1996 it has been possible for trade mark owners to file for a registered Community trade mark (CTM) and through just one application to achieve trade mark protection simultaneously in all 15 countries of the European Community, namely:

- Austria
- Belgium
- Denmark
- Finland
- France
- Germany
- Greece
- Ireland
- Italy
- Luxembourg
- Netherlands
- Portugal
- Spain
- Sweden
- United Kingdom.

To file an application for a Community trade mark (initially valid for 10 years and renewable thereafter indefinitely, subject to the mark's commercial use), official registration forms (or electronic application form on 3.5″ diskette) and trade mark representations can be filed either through the national trade mark office or directly to the Office for the Harmonisation of the Internal Market (Trade Marks and Designs) known as OHIM based in Alicante/Spain.

Through the latest UK Trade Marks Act 1994 ratifications were implemented to meet the requirements of new EU trade mark legislation. In effect, this means that the legal structure and trade mark criteria are equivalent between the UK legislation TMA 1994 and the Community trade mark (refer to section 5.3).

Although in processing CTM applications the national office in Britain—the Patent Office—will only be involved in the following:

- recording the application, the date of receipt and the number of pages;
- despatching the application forms promptly to Alicante by courier;
- providing an acknowledgement of date of receipt, applicant's reference, number of attachments, number of pages despatched to OHIM and the handling fee received.

Examination and registration itself will be made by the central OHIM office, which will contact the applicant/representative directly in respect of any problems or omissions. Similarly, the national office will only receive the handling fee whilst the registration fee payable in ECUs must be sent directly to OHIM.

Non-EU companies and brand name owners, who wish to obtain a Community trade mark should file their application through an EU-based representative directly to OHIM. The official languages of OHIM are English, French, German, Italian and Spanish—with English likely to be the most widely used.

Priority claim from national trade mark registration

If a trade mark application is already filed at national level, the owner can (within the first six months) use the date of the first application for the purpose of claiming priority of a mark.

While it is not a requirement for a Community trade mark to be based upon a national registration, a brand name user may wish to achieve European registration/protection from the outset. However, one should still carry out a search among existing trade mark registrations to avoid wasting time and resources if a similar or even the same brand name is already registered or otherwise protected, e.g. through 'first use' claim of an unregistered mark—in the UK or other EU Member States.

Once a Community trade mark is registered—following similar procedures to a national application in the UK—the registration will be published for opposition purposes in the monthly '*Community Trade Marks Bulletin*'. Although all applications undergo initial examination and search procedures against existing trade marks registrations, the OHIM will not object to registration on the basis of conflict from its own volition. That is up to the individual trade mark owners taking action. So, it is advisable for trade mark owners to monitor and keep up to date with all new trade mark applications published in the EU bulletin, to ensure no confusingly similar trade mark is registered in the same or similar goods to an existing registration.

For further information and application forms for Community trade mark registration, refer to the OHIM address list at the end of this book.

7.5 Design protection in the EU

With intellectual property legislation within EU countries having developed very differently according to national borders and the wishes of individual countries, design protection means different things in most European countries which, through lack of one European design protection system, can make it difficult for original design owners within the clothing and fashion industries to achieve effective (cost and time) design protection for original designs.

Before looking at the Community design regulations due for EU implementation in the very near future, it may be interesting to consider how different the existing design protections are throughout the EU countries.

In France, for example, most industrial designs can qualify for copyright protection, whereas in the UK clear distinctions only allow *artistic* works to obtain copyright while industrial design is covered by the automatic design right. Whereas in Portugal pattern designs applied to industrially-produced products do not qualify for copyright, but may instead qualify for design registration valid for one year (renewable indefinitely) provided the form or ornamental aspects include novelty. In comparison, a UK design registration will be valid for five years and renewable for a maximum of 25 years. Presumably the UK design registration involves less time and paperwork in maintaining the registration compared to yearly registration renewal.

In the instance of registered design protection other examples include Denmark and Germany where the maximum protection term is 15 years, whilst Greek legislation offers no design protection at all for ornamental and/or industrial design.

Then, there is the aspect of the one design falling into different national protection categories, depending on function, aesthetics and other elements of the article whereby some countries classify utility articles as qualifying as 'petty patents' or 'utility models' with varying definitions and protection terms. Therefore, in the past it has quite rightly been regarded by designers and businesses as too complex, expensive and time-consuming both to obtain protection and take legal action against infringements on a European level. Although successfully defending original designs overseas has not been impossible, as shown in the following case study.

CASE STUDY

French copyright test case (1993)

A British knitwear design company won the right to stop the copying of its garments in a French copyright infringement action, following over one year of legal action costing about £8,000. It won damages of around £18,000 but more importantly it was one of the first UK companies to win a case against a Paris fashion house in the French courts.

The beginning of this legal victory started in Paris in spring 1991, when the designer spotted an almost identical copy of one of her garments in the Paris show-room of a French customer. The version on display was an inferior machine knit copy as opposed to the designer's hand-knits. But flickers of suspicion were fanned into flames when a week or so later the Paris fashion house made it clear it would no longer be sourcing products from the UK company.

It was hoped that an infringing copy from the defendant company would turn up in a UK outlet, as this would automatically bring the problem under English juris-diction. But there was no such luck—copies appeared everywhere but in the UK. However, by late summer there were reports of the copies seen for sale in the USA and in France. On her next visit to New York the original designer went into one of the major department stores and purchased an infringing copy from the Paris fash-ion house's concession. Having returned to the UK, legal preparation of evidence and tactics were undertaken but the action could only be brought in France, under French law.

With some clever detection work involving a hidden camera, and armed with a copy of the infringing garment purchased in New York and another purchased from a French outlet, the designer and English lawyer met with a French counsel, an expert in French intellectual property law.

Following the lawyer's advice to prove originality, the UK lawyer prepared a dossier with affidavits and exhibits showing photographs of original prototypes, current copy products, supporting evidence of the dates and originality of the photog-raphs, as well as independent newspaper and magazine articles which demonstrated the originality of her client's design, drawing and toile. Also, they were advised to provide evidence of the strong legal support and protection English law would have given the designer had the infringement occurred in the UK due to reciprocity rules to interchange privileges between countries.

In addition, a catalogue from the defending company was obtained, which revealed a colour photograph of an almost exact replica of the design company's popular and well-defined cardigan/jackets. This was a deciding factor in the case, together with the British lawyer's statement on the English law giving the French lawyers confidence to proceed.

On Christmas Eve 1991, the French court officers made a surprise raid on the company's premises and seized further copies of garments and various papers. Unlike in the UK, police authority is needed for a seizure. There is also a special court in Paris for infringements and the charge subject also includes a criminal element, as the French are keen to protect design generally, and haute couture especially.

Once the litigation wheels began to turn the case took about nine months to come to the Palais de Justice. A month later, judgement in favour of the UK designer was delivered.

The essence of an action of this kind is to compel the infringer to cease copying your original design product for two reasons: eroding your existing market and damaging your reputation and thus affecting your future market. In any successful action, there must be clear and independent evidence of originality and dates, possibly of every early drawing and prototypes which designers and intellectual property owners should keep for all their works.

The outcome of this case should encourage smaller companies whose best selling designs are being ripped off. Redress from the courts is available across national borders, in this instance outside the UK—even if the infringing copies are not on sale in the designer's own country.

Reproduced with the permission of Drapers Record, © January 30, 1993

When viewing the various national systems for intellectual property it rapidly becomes clear that definitions of design, legitimacy and the duration of protection in EU Member States are as diverse as the industrial rudiments of each Member State, representing approximately nine different sets of IP regulations. It becomes apparent why substantial time is required to negotiate new Community design regulations which can operate satisfactorily in all Member States.

For comparisons of the maximum term of protection of registered design under current national legislations in different European countries see Figure 7.1. Similar comparative illustrations could be drawn up for other intellectual property rights, e.g. copyright, petty patents and trade marks, to show the diversity of national jurisdictions.

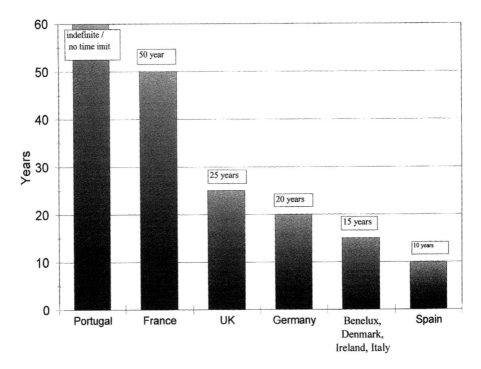

Figure 7.1 Registered design duration via national legislations in the EU

The problem in *not* establishing common market protection, is that whilst goods may move freely between states, protection systems only apply nationally. A design heavily protected in one country may have little or no protection in another. Also, even if national laws could be harmonised, intellectual property registration would continue to only apply in the country where protection is granted—not moving with the design as it is being sold within EU trading countries. Therefore, protection of industrial design at European Community level will help prevent counterfeiting and strengthen the Community's added value.

Until the early 1990s even the European Commission considered the legislation regarding intellectual property and protection rights on a European level so complex, that to produce a common system would take up too much time and too many resources, whereas recent EU developments with the introduction of a Community trade mark and the proposed regulation for Community designs indicates that considerable progress has been made from which design and branded goods industries will be able to fully benefit sooner rather than later, with protection throughout the European Community for original intellectual property— without the national legislative distortions between EU Member States.

7.6 New European legislation for Community design protection

One of the prime objectives set out by the European Community Treaty focuses on the continued work which will be 'ensuring the economic and social progress of the Community countries by common action to elim-inate the barriers which divide Europe . . . ' with the purpose of the inter-nal market to ensure the 'abolition of obstacles to the free movement of goods and the institution of a system ensuring that competition in the common market is not distorted . . . '.

As illustrated through the examples of different national IP legislation between EU countries these diverse systems inevitably lead to conflicts between Member States, an element which constitutes an obstacle to the free movement of goods. Hence, the establishment of a Community design system which offers uniform protection throughout the EU is seen as greatly improving and strengthening the internal market both within Community countries and towards non-EU countries. Once a Community design system is operating it may also become a strong negotiation tool for starting to seek corresponding design protection in the most important export markets of the European Community.

With improved legislation, designers and industries are likely to be encouraged to incorporate higher levels of development and investment to distinguish their products through strong, innovative design in the market-place and to strengthen the European Community's added value. The element of superior design is seen as an important attribute of EU industries in competition with industries from other countries and is, in many cases, a decisive factor for commercial success. Therefore, improved design protection will benefit not only the individual design but improve the European Community's competitiveness on a macro-economic level.

The proposed EU Regulation for Community design (see Bibliography for details) aims to strongly simplify the process of register-ing designs with one application and processing procedure covering the whole of the EU with protection lasting for a maximum of up to 25 years through renewal of individual five-year terms. By operating under one design system, legal action across the Community will also benefit greatly from the new legislation and generally improve business competition.

The focus of the Community design Regulation reveals that the European Council considers it unnecessary to undertake a full-scale approximation of the design laws of EU Member States. Instead it will be sufficient if the approximation is limited to those national provisions of law which most directly affect the functioning of the internal market, while provisions on sanctions, remedies and enforcement are likely to be left to national law. In other words the conditions for obtaining a registered design right will be identical in all the EU Member States.

7.7 Community design definition

First of all it is necessary to establish exactly what constitutes 'design' to ensure the same interpretation is used throughout EU Member States, hence the following official descriptions:

1. *'Design'* means the appearance of the whole or a part of a product resulting from the features of, in particular, the lines, contours, colours, shape, texture and/or materials of the product itself and/or its ornamentation.
2. *'Product'* means any industrial or handicraft item, including parts intended to be assembled into a complex product, packaging, get-ups, graphic symbols and typographic typefaces (but excluding computer programs).
3. *'Complex product'* means a product which is composed of multiple components which can be replaced permitting disassembly and reassembly of the product.

The definition made in the EU Regulation, for the type of designs which can make use of the Community design system, include the following requirements to be fulfilled:

The design must be *new* and have an *individual character.*

New meaning 'in the sense that it is not identical to any other design previously made available to the public' this is to fulfil the requirement of *novelty*. Designs will be considered to be identical if their features differ only in immaterial details.

The overall impression of novelty and individual character of a design should be viewed as it would be perceived by an informed user, and from that aspect must be seen to differ significantly from the overall impression produced on such a user by any other existing design, taking into account the nature of the product and the industrial sector to which it belongs. In addition, the degree of freedom of the designer in developing the design shall be taken into consideration.

Excluded designs include designs identical to an existing or already published design. Should two designs and their particular features differ only in immaterial details, they will be deemed 'identical' and therefore fail to represent a *new/novelty* element.

Other particular designs which will be excluded from the EU protection system will include: designs produced purely to meet functional requirements, allowing no arbitrary design features, e.g. designs of mechanical fittings or spare parts (categories less likely to apply to the textile and clothing industries).

7.8 Unregistered and registered Community design

In trying to establish legislation which will meet the design requirements of all industries and products with different product life cycles, the EU consulted various industries, governmental and independent organisations and, as a result, the need for two types of Community designs have been identified.

For sectors which produce large quantities of designs with comparatively short life cycles there is the need for a protection system which allows design protection without the burden of registration formalities and where the duration of protection is of a lesser significance. On the other hand there are industries which do require the greater legal certainty of a formal registration system and longer terms of protection. As a result establishing two forms of protection is necessary.

One is a short-term *unregistered design right* and the other is a longer term *registered design right*, both categories of rights to be dealt with as an object of property which applies for the whole area of the European Community and as strongly as a national design right in the individual Member State.

Unregistered Community design rights will provide the right to prevent copying and/or the trade in products infringing the design for a period of three years. Registered Community design rights will give the owner *exclusive* rights of the design and consist of greater legal certainty, also giving the right to prevent third parties from using the design with-out consent. A registration application must be filed within the first year of marketing/publication. Initially, the design protection term will be valid for five years and may be renewed up to a maximum of 25 years by renewal of the Community design registration every five years.

7.9 Design ownership rights

The ownership of a Community design will belong to the creator/designer. In the instance of a design being created as part of the normal duties of an employee—or the product of specific instructions given by his/her employer—the right to the Community design shall belong to the employer, unless otherwise provided by contract. If a design is the product of joint development among a team of designers, ownership rights will belong jointly to all in the team.

While the name(s) of the applicant or official holder of a registered Community design may belong to an employer the European regulations provide *specific rights of the designer*. In recognising the creative input by designers—be it as individuals or part of a design team—designers are given the right to be cited as such before the Community design office or in the register.

Where two identical designs have been created independently (not copied) *unregistered designs* will share the ownership rights of that design, while maintaining the rights to prevent others from copying or infringing the design through producing, selling, importing, exporting or stocking copies. In the case of registered Community design, exclusive ownership rights will generally belong to the individual/company who first files its application—the same applying during the *period of grace* (see definition in following section 7.10). One exception includes the situation where a third party can prove that he has '*rights of prior use*'. In such cases the third party must prove that before the date of any design application was filed, he had already created the same design independently (not through copying) and in good faith started or made serious preparations to start publishing the design within the EU.

The aspect of encouraging designers and/or owners to register designs as early as possible to avoid any design rights being pre-empted by other applications, to some extent pre-empts the function of the 12-month period of grace. However, it is important that the Community design system strikes a balance between exclusive protection systems that are too restrictive to allow a healthy level of competition in the European market-place.

Ownership rights, similar to IP rights in the United Kingdom, are treated as standard business assets which may be transferred, sold or licensed. In relation to Community design licence agreements, rights can be negotiated for the whole or only part of the EU and can be exclusive or non-exclusive to the licensee. Any agreements regarding the transfer or granting of licensing rights for a registered Community design must be entered in the central register and published.

In cases of *alleged infringements*, the licensee may bring proceedings against a defendant, only if the owner of a Community design right consents thereto although the holder of exclusive licensing rights will be allowed to bring infringement proceedings himself if the Community design owner has been given notice of the infringements and does not himself bring legal action within an appropriate period.

Where legal infringement action is brought by the Community design holder, a licensee will be entitled to intervene in the action to present a compensation claim for damages suffered by him through the infringement.

7.10 Period of grace

This new concept already introduced at the 'Green Paper' stage of the legislative development, allows the designer (or design owners) to test the products embodying the design in the market place for a period of 12 months, before deciding whether it is desirable to obtain more long-term protection through a registered Community design.

The one-year period of grace—for initial market testing—will typically be useful to companies or designers publishing numerous designs each year or season, as is often the case for fashion companies. After one year the company can then narrow down the choice and decide which products to spend time and cost on for registration or whether it is sufficient to continue with an unregistered design right.

Making use of the one-year period of grace will not affect the registration assessment of a design's novelty and individual character. However, the application for registration of a Community design must be filed within the 12-month period of publishing and/or marketing design(s).

7.11 Registered Community design

Whereas unregistered design protection is applicable for short-term designs such as high fashion companies giving automatic protection for up to three years for original designs, the registration system is targeted at design articles which require a more long-term protection. Once registered the Community design may be renewed at the request of the right holder for one or more periods of five years, up to a total term of 25 years from the date of filing design application.

It is a fundamental objective of the EU design system that registration must present the minimum difficulty and cost to applicants, to make it readily available to small and medium-sized companies as well as individual designers. Also, to accommodate sectors which produce large numbers of designs over a short period of time, the application system is planned to include the option of combining a number of designs in one multiple application. It has been suggested to allow as many as 100 designs to be filed in one application, a number easily accommodating the needs of most European fashion companies.

With the introduction of the period of grace a company's design will benefit from the automatic Community design protection, allowing for the design or a range of designs to be market tested and their initial success assessed before deciding whether to proceed with and obtain the exclusive rights through a registered Community design, which clearly has a higher degree of protection. This structure seems to present very sound benefits both for industrial design products and the commercial business environment, be it for small or large-scale production.

7.12 Central structure for Community design

As well as processing and granting design rights through the Community design register, the central structure will also consist of a specialised division dealing with copying, ownership disputes and general legal matters, with jurisdiction throughout the EU concerning Community design.

The central Community design offices will consist of the following main divisions:

- Formalities Examination Division;
- Design Administration;

- Legal Division;
- Invalidity Division.

The central divisions will be supported throughout the EU Member States who must set up a limited number of specialised Community design courts.

7.13 Application procedure

For an application to be considered for registration, general requirements include that the design must either already be commercialised in the market-place at the date of application (e.g. having made use of the 12-month period of grace available before applications must be filed). Alternatively, the design must be published following Community registration or still be benefitting from national design protection in an EU Member State, provided the national protection has not expired at the date of filing the application for Community design.

Completed applications can be filed either directly with the Community Design Office—likely to be the OHIM office (Office for Harmonisation in the Internal Market) based in Alicante, Spain—and already the central office for Community trade mark registrations. Alternatively, the application can be filed through the central industrial property office in each EU country.

Applications will consist of standard documents, indicating the applicant and designer(s) responsible for the creation, plus the appropriate registration fees. Further information will include details such as:

- representation and description of the design(s);
- product categories in which the design(s) will apply;
- specimen or sample of the design(s);
- possible request for deferment of publication of the application.

Under the Paris Convention agreement, applicants for Community designs can request the '*right of priority*', provided applications for the same design have been filed in other Paris Convention countries within the previous six months of filing for Community design, and provided the first application has not been withdrawn, abandoned or refused.

7.14 Publication of Community design

Once the application has been filed, the registration office will examine that all requirements are satisfied for a Community design, e.g. elements of novelty and distinctiveness are met and all documents are complete and the fees have been paid in full.

Upon registration the Community design will be published in the *Community Design Bulletin*, identifying:

- the right holder;
- the number and date of filing application (or the priority date);
- the citation of the designer or design team;
- the design representation;
- a reference to where a specimen or sample has been filed.

Deferment of publication

The actual necessity of publishing design registrations has been examined at the very early stages of the legislative development, and very valid reasons have been identified for delaying the publication of a design registration;

1. Due to the lack of exhaustive validation, caused by the existence of *unregistered* designs within the EC, publication of registered design applications cannot guarantee total design right.
2. The overall cost of the application including a publication will be higher compared to applications without the publication fee.
3. Publication may in fact greatly facilitate the use of the design for pirating and copying.

As the full publication will include design representations and the exposure risk towards pirating—especially in fast-moving sectors such as the fashion industry—the introduction of publication deferment is a particularly welcome move by the EU Regulation. At the stage of filing application, the request for deferment of publication will be made by the applicant, not exceeding 30 months. When the EU-wide registration is granted neither the representation of the design nor any file relating to the application shall be open to public inspection. Instead, publication will only be made identifying the right holder, the date of filing and the length of the deferment period.

This non-publication structure is subject to a third party being able to prove *a legitimate interest* in an application, for example if original ownership rights are disputed or there are instances of alleged infringement by the applicant. Providing a person can establish a legitimate interest in the design application or registration, he may inspect a file without the consent of an applicant or the right holder of the registered Community design.

At the expiry of deferment, or earlier if requested by the right holder, all entries in the central register will be open to public inspection.

7.15 Summary

With the increased economic integration of the European countries it would seem only logical that the single market should operate one Community design protection legislation rather than numerous sets of national laws.

The obvious advantages of common EU legislation are visible through the Community trade mark legislation enforced in January 1996. The CTM is applied as the common foundation for each EU Member State to bring its own trade mark law up to date within the same legal structure and trade mark criteria thereby making it substantially easier for trade mark owners in future to protect their brand names and take legal action if necessary throughout the EU when exporting to other member countries.

For the purpose of protecting original design concepts, substantial legislative developments are taking place on a European scale. The EU Regulation is likely in the imminent future to establish protection for a Community design system, subject to a formal review, analysis and possible improvements by the European Commission five years after the legislative implementation, in order to assess the functioning for EU industry, consumers, competition and the internal market overall.

The new design protection will introduce unregistered design rights similar to UK design rights, though the EU version limits protection to three years. All designs which are to benefit from Community design rights must satisfy certain requirements of representing new and distinctive designs.

A period of grace for the first 12 months of a design publication/product marketing, will allow companies to market test designs prior to Community design registration. This concept gives companies and/or design owners the opportunity to assess a design's commercial value and

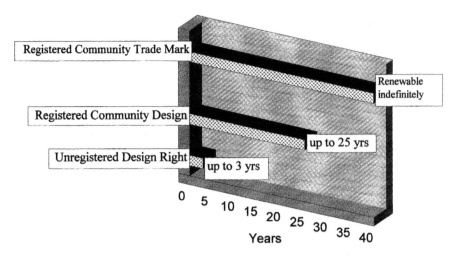

Registered Community Trade Mark

Renewable indefinitely

Registered Community Design

up to 25 yrs

Unregistered Design Right

up to 3 yrs

0 5 10 15 20 25 30 35 40

Years

Figure 7.2 EU intellectual property protection (current and proposed EU legislation)

decide either to strengthen the design protection through registration or whether the unregistered design, valid for three years, will be sufficient for the product's life cycle.

Should a design prove to be particularly successful within the period of grace, the more long-term design protection from a Community design registration may be required. Whereas, unregistered original designs only obtain the right of preventing others from copying or otherwise infringing the design, a registration will grant the holder exclusive design ownership rights. The initial registration will be valid for five years and renewable up to a maximum of 25 years.

8

THE WTO AGREEMENT FOR INTELLECTUAL PROPERTY: TRIPS

8.1 The WTO Agreement

The World Trade Organisation—WTO—was established in January 1995 as a result of the concluded Uruguay Round. In effect, the WTO is the successor of the international GATT structure which prime objective concerned the General Agreement on Tariffs and Trade.

Since the first GATT agreement in 1947, subsequent Trade Rounds in 1949, 1951, 1956 and 1961 focused entirely on the subject of tariffs and the updated agreements more or less remained the same as in 1947. Only during the trade conventions held in 1967 and 1979 did new areas such as anti-dumping measures and 'framework' agreements become part of the international debate.

When the Uruguay Round was initiated in 1986, international commerce and world economy had already developed into much more complex industries which required the debate and structures of much wider issues than trading tariffs, to meet the needs of businesses trading internationally.

Subjects covered in this latest trade agreement have therefore been extended to the following: tariffs, non-tariff measures, rules, services, dispute settlement, agriculture, textiles and clothing, establishment of the new World Trade Organisation (WTO) structure—and for the first time; Intellectual property rights.

The Uruguay Round was signed by no less than 123 countries (see Box 8.1) and recognised not only as the biggest negotiation mandate on trade ever agreed, but also seen as 'the anchor for development and an instrument of economic and trade reform'.

In order to support this much wider spectrum of worldwide collaboration, in terms of the commercial activity and trade policies for international trade, a new system has been created under the WTO. The highest authority of the WTO is the Ministerial Conference, taking place every two years. The actual day-to-day work of the WTO takes place in various subsidiary bodies such as:

- General Council;
- Dispute Settlement Body;
- Trade Policy Review Body;
  - Council for Trade in Goods;
  - Council for Trade in Services;
  - Council for Trade-Related Aspects of Intellectual Property Rights.

In connection to intellectual property the specialised Council for Trade-Related Aspects of Intellectual Property Rights now exists on a permanent basis. Other sections of the new WTO structure which are of interest to the clothing and textile industry in other fields of international trade include the Textiles Monitoring Body, the Committee on Rules of Origin, the Committee on Import Licensing and the Dispute Settlement Body.

With the establishment of the central and permanent WTO organisation (based in Geneva), with a secretariat and much wider council structure in place, significant changes have taken place. A much broader scope than GATT is now applied by WTO, in terms of commercial activity and trade policies.

Direct access to the WTO can be made on the World Wide Web, where the home page of WTO is found under: http://www.unicc.org/wto/. In addition to a constantly updated list of the TRIPs country members, general information which may be of interest is located at the WTO web site. In the near future Internet users will be able to access a large amount of WTO documentation.

8.2 The TRIPs agreement

The particular part of the GATT 1994 agreement dealing with IP protection and legislative structures is the agreement on Trade-Related Aspects of Intellectual Property Rights—known as the TRIPs agreement (see Bibliography for details).

The overall purpose of the international IP agreement is 'to promote

Box 8.1

Member countries of the World Trade Organisation (WTO)

(123 countries as of July 1996)

Antigua/Barbuda	EC	Luxembourg	Saint Vincent
Argentina	Ecuador	Macau	and the
Australia	Egypt	Madagascar	Grenadines
Austria	El Salvador	Malawi	Senegal
Bahrain	Fiji	Malaysia	Sierra Leone
Bangladesh	Finland	Maldives	Singapore
Barbados	France	Mali	Slovak Republic
Belgium	Gabon	Malta	Slovenia
Belize	Germany	Mauritania	Solomon Islands
Benin	Ghana	Mauritius	South Africa
Bolivia	Greece	Mexico	Spain
Botswana	Grenada	Morocco	Sri Lanka
Brazil	Guatemala	Mozambique	Surinam
Brunei	Guinea Bissau	Myanmar	Swaziland
Darussalam	Guinea, Rep. of	Namibia	Sweden
Burkina Faso	Guyana	Netherlands	Switzerland
Burundi	Haiti	New Zealand	Tanzania
Cameroon	Honduras	Nicaragua	Thailand
Canada	Hong Kong	Nigeria	Togo
Central African	Hungary	Norway	Trinidad and
Republic	Iceland	Pakistan	Tobago
Chile	India	Papua New	Tunisia
Colombia	Indonesia	Guinea	Turkey
Costa Rica	Ireland	Paraguay	Uganda
Cote d'Ivoire	Israel	Peru	United Arab
Cuba	Italy	Philippines	Emirates
Cyprus	Jamaica	Poland	United Kingdom
Czech Republic	Japan	Portugal	Uruguay
Denmark	Kenya	Qatar	USA
Djibouti	Korea	Romania	Venezuela
Dominica	Kuwait	Rwanda	Zambia
Dominican	Lesotho	Saint Kitts/Nevis	Zimbabwe
Rep.	Liechtenstein	Saint Lucia	

Observer governments (37) of the WTO

Albania	Bulgaria	Croatia	Gambia
Algeria	Cambodia	Estonia	Georgia
Angola	Chad	Former Yugoslav	Jordan
Armenia	China	Rep. of	Kazakhstan
Belarus	Congo	Macedonia	Kyrgyz Rep.

Latvia	Niger	Saudi Arabia	Ukraine
Lithuania	Oman	Seychelles	Uzbekistan
Moldova	Panama	Sudan	Vanuatu
Mongolia	Russian	Taipei, Chinese	Vietnam
Nepal	Federation	Tonga	Zaire

effective and adequate protection of intellectual property rights, and to ensure that measures and procedures to enforce intellectual property rights do not themselves become barriers to legitimate trade'. Furthermore 'The protection and enforcement of intellectual property rights should contribute to the promotion of technological innovation and to the transfer and dissemination of technology, to the mutual advantage of producers and users of technological knowledge and in a manner conducive to social and economic welfare, and to a balance of rights and obligations'.

Whilst taking into account the differences of national IP legislations, the agreement aims to ensure that provision is made in membership countries for effective prevention of infringements and the establishment of settlement structures to solve disputes and trade-related intellectual property issues through multilateral procedures.

To implement and monitor the progress of the TRIPs agreement the WTO will be co-operating with the World Intellectual Property Organisation (WIPO) as well as other relevant international organisations.

Basic principles

The TRIPs agreement establishes the minimum legal requirements, IP rights and principles to which membership countries must adhere, although developing countries will be allowed a transitional term of four years, subject to the monitoring of the Council of TRIPs to ensure satisfactory progress is taking place in the country concerned.

Any new national legislation coming into force after signing the WTO agreement must not be obstructive to the provisions of the TRIPs agreement, and as the agreement structures present the minimum requirements new national law can of course exceed the TRIPs standards.

Similar to both UK and EU legislative frameworks 'intellectual property' is recognised as private rights and includes all IP categories:

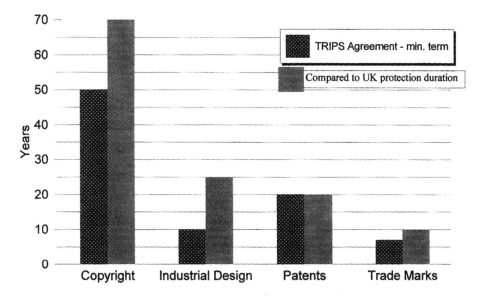

Note: Trade Mark durations illustrate the initial protection term, renewable indefinitely both under TRIPS and UK legislation, subject to use of the trade mark.

Figure 8.1 International TRIPs agreement: minimum protection term/duration

- copyrights and related rights;
- trade marks (for both products and services);
- industrial designs;
- patents;
- protection of undisclosed information.

The treatment of intellectual property and right owners as laid out by the international agreement shall extend not only to a country's own nationals, but to nationals of *all* other member countries, allowing them to make use of national procedures and registration rights available in the individual country. The equal treatment, in legal terms, of all Member States' nationals establishes the same criteria as applied for other international IP agreements such as the Paris Convention (1967) and the Berne Convention (1971). It should be noted, however, that the TRIPs agreement does not replace the existing obligations of other conventions but its provisions are to be implemented in 'addition to' any earlier agreements.

The following sections outline the application of the TRIPs agreement to various types of intellectual property, in several instances the legal framework and IP definitions are highly similar to IP rights as found both in the European Community rights and the legislative structure in the UK.

8.3 Copyright and related rights

The TRIPs copyright protection extends to expressions, e.g. artistic and literary works but does not include ideas, procedures, methods of operation or mathematical concepts.

Exceptions which will normally qualify for copyright protection are computer programs (both in source and object code) as well as compilations of data or other material, which through the selection or arrangement of their contents, constitute *intellectual creations*.

Rights of the copyright holder—be it the author or his successor in title—include the right to authorise or alternatively prevent the commercial use of his work without prior consent.

Term of protection

In cases where the copyright protection is not related to the life span of the creator/author, the term of protection must be no less than 50 years following the year of publication.

In comparison, the existing UK copyright term is considerably longer at 70 years.

8.4 Trade marks

The TRIPs definition of protectable subject-matter in this category of intellectual property is as follows: any sign or any combination of signs, capable of distinguishing the goods or services of one undertaking from those of other undertakings.

The trade mark words can include personal names, letters, numerals, figurative elements, combinations of colours and/or signs although qualifying for registration as a trade mark in the TRIPs countries may depend on the brand name *distinctiveness*, be it acquired through use or inherently distinctive. Countries may also establish the registration condition that signs must be capable of being visually illustrated.

Once registered, the ownership rights of a trade mark shall give the *exclusive right* to prevent all third parties from using an *identical* mark or a *similar sign* for goods or services in the course of trade, be it for *identical* or *similar* goods/services as used for the registered trade mark. Although, as in the UK system, this will not prejudice any existing rights for say a minor local company which may have used the same or a similar brand name for a period of time and locally to have become known as trading under the particular brand, in which instance the local business has some claim of rights through prior use.

Equal to the EU and UK trade mark registration systems, member states of the international TRIPs systems must publish each trade mark either before it is registered or immediately after granting ownership rights. Following publication a reasonable amount of time shall be allowed for petitions from third parties to challenge the registration.

Requirement of use

A country may require that a registered trade mark is being actively used in commercial trade, although an application must not be refused purely on the grounds that the brand is not used commercially at the time of application. Neither must the requirements for use of a trade mark present an unjustifiable burden through special requirements.

Only after a period of three years from the date of filing an application will the TRIPs agreement allow for a trade mark registration to be revoked due to lack of commercial use unless valid reasons based on the existence of independent obstacles can support the reasons for non-use, e.g. import restrictions or other government requirements for goods or services protected by the trade mark, which will be recognised as valid reasons for non-use.

Term of protection

The initial registration and any following renewal for a trade mark must be no less than seven years. The registration of a trade mark shall be renewable indefinitely. In comparison the term of protection both for a British and Community trade mark registration is 10 years, also renewable indefinitely.

Trade mark licensing

Within the TRIPs agreement it is understood that compulsory licensing of a trade mark will not be permitted and owners of trade marks have the right to assign the brand name with or without the transfer of the business to which the trade mark belongs.

Geographical indications of trade marks

For geographical indications (e.g. Shetland Wool, Egyptian Cotton, etc.)—used for goods or services to identify the place of origin, be it a country, a region or locality in a geographical area where a certain quality, reputation or other characteristic of the product/service is attributed, the geographical indication or use of any means in the designation or presentation must be the true place of origin, in other words the indication of origin must be of such nature as not to mislead the public.

A trade mark containing misleading indications of the place of origin will qualify for application refusal for trade mark registrations or result in the registration being invalidated.

8.5 Industrial designs

The requirements are for all TRIPs countries to provide for 'the protection of independently created industrial designs that are new or original'. Designs must differ significantly from known designs or a combination of known design features although protection shall not extend to designs essentially dictated by technical or functional elements.

In the agreement for industrial design protection special attention is given to the textile industry by stating that: 'Each member (state) shall ensure that requirements for securing protection for textile designs, in particular in regard to any cost, examination or publication, do not unreasonably impair the opportunity to seek and obtain such (industrial design) protection'. The obligation can be accommodated by countries through industrial design law or through copyright law.

Intellectual property protection for industrial designs will give the right to prevent third parties from making, selling or importing articles bearing or embodying a design which is a copy, be it a complete or *substantial* copy for commercial purposes.

Term of protection

For industrial design articles the duration of protection available in TRIPs member countries must be at least 10 years although note that the design protection is not achieved directly from the TRIPs agreement *itself*, it is the responsibility of signatory countries of the agreement to make provisions for the 10-year protection period within their national design legislation.

Notably, this time-scale of 10 years' protection is considerably less than current registered design in the UK and the Community design system developing for the EC market, both providing up to 25 years of design protection although it may be argued that for many fashion and textile companies the international 10-year protection term will prove sufficient.

8.6 Patents

With patent registration being the intellectual property category most established through previous international conventions, the structure for patent protection within the TRIPs agreement is more or less identical to existing patent specifications.

Patents will be available for all technological inventions, whether they are products or processes, provided that they are *new*, involve an *inventive step* and are *capable of industrial application* (refer to Chapter 5, dealing with the identical UK patent criteria).

The patent will give the owner exclusive rights to prevent other parties, without the patent holder's consent, from making, using, offering for sale, selling or importing the patented product. Also the patent holder shall have the right to assign, transfer or license the patent.

Procedures and information requirements for filing applications, followed by publication are, in general, structured similarly to existing international patent processing.

Term of protection

The total term of protection available for patents in TRIPs member countries must be no less than 20 years (the same term as applied in the UK and existing international patent convention agreements).

Burden of proof

In cases of patent disputes, the burden of proof will be required by the defendant. The accused party will be required to prove satisfactorily that the process to obtain an identical product is different from the patented process. If the alleged infringer fails to provide satisfactory proof to the contrary, it will be ruled that the unauthorised patent product applied the patented process to arrive at the same product.

8.7 Protection of undisclosed information

Under the TRIPs agreement provisions are made for natural and legal persons to prevent information lawfully within their control from being disclosed to, acquired by or used by others without their consent, normally used in honest commercial trade, provided that:

1. The information is secret, e.g. the precise configuration and assembly of components is not readily available or generally known to individuals normally working in the particular industry or intellectual property field.
2. The information is of commercial value, because it is secret.
3. The person in control of the information has taken reasonable steps to protect the information and maintain the secrecy.

8.8 Enforcement of IP rights—general obligations

Signatory countries of the agreement must ensure that effective enforcement procedures are established to allow intellectual property owners action against any type of infringement, as well as functioning as sufficient deterrent remedies against possible counterfeit operations, in particular by preventing the entry of infringing and counterfeit articles into the channels of commerce within their jurisdiction, through the interception of imported goods immediately after customs clearance as well as preserving relevant evidence in regard to the alleged infringement, particularly where there is a demonstrable risk of evidence being destroyed, which is likely to cause irreparable harm to the right holder.

However, any such procedures must operate in a manner which avoids the creation of barriers for legitimate trade while at the same time safeguarding against abuse of intellectual property rights.

Procedures for intellectual property should not be cumbersome, unnecessarily complicated or present unreasonable time limits and delays. For legal proceedings, decisions must be reasoned and available in writing, at least to the parties involved in a dispute. Where an initial judicial decision has been made, opportunities must be available for a review of the case merits by a final judicial instance.

Evidence

In connection with legal action the judicial authorities are given the right to order the defendant to produce evidence of defence, similar to the burden of evidence described earlier in the TRIPs patent section. Should the alleged infringer fail to provide evidence, the appropriate court will have the authority to make preliminary and final determinations based on the evidence presented to them by the intellectual property owner bringing the action.

Injunctions

The official legal authorities will have the right to order a party to desist from infringement to prevent the entry of counterfeit goods into commercial channels within the country of jurisdiction. The action of injunction should provide the legal authorities with the ability to block the release of alleged counterfeit goods immediately after customs clearance.

In cases where counterfeit products were acquired or ordered by a person prior to knowing, or having reasonable grounds to know, that dealing in the products would constitute an action of infringement of intellectual property, judicial authorities may limit the infringement remedies available to payment of remuneration or adequate compensation for the intellectual property owner.

Damages

The authority must be available to order the infringer to pay damages adequate to compensate the right holder for the injury of infringement plus the legal expenses in connection with the action taken. Courts may also be given the authority to order the recovery of profits and/or damages, even when the infringer did not knowingly become involved in infringing activities.

Court orders disposing of infringing goods

As part of establishing effective anti-copying deterrent systems, judicial authorities shall have the power to order the destruction or disposal of goods found to be infringing without any form of compensation to the infringer. Destruction/disposal orders will also include the material and main components used to produce infringing articles.

The purpose of this action is to minimise the risks of further and/or repeat infringement. Hence, in cases of counterfeit trade mark articles, the simple removal of the unlawful copy trade mark label(s) will not be sufficient action, apart from in exceptional cases, simply because it would be too easy for such trade mark copies to re-enter and find their way back into commercial channels.

The disposal of infringing products must take place outside the channels of commerce and must not present any harm to the official right holder whilst the request or need for such court orders should be in proportion to the seriousness of the infringement, viewed together with other remedies ordered by the court.

Right of information

Legal authorities will be able to order the infringer to inform the right holder of the identity of third parties involved in the production and distribution of infringing goods as well as their channels of distribution thereby allowing the owner(s) of intellectual property to get to the root of infringement operations.

Abuse of enforcement procedures

Legal measures or actions taken which, at a later date, are found to represent wrongful or false accusations of infringement, or in other ways having abused the enforcement procedures will result in penalties. The legal authority can, in such instances, order the applicant to pay adequate compensation for the injury suffered by the alleged defendant—including appropriate legal expenses. Exception to such penalty will be allowed where public authorities and officials acted in good faith.

Provisional measures to legal action

Before legal measures, e.g. injunction orders, are granted the applicant may be required to provide any reasonable available evidence in order to satisfy the authorities and to establish a sufficient degree of certainty that the applicant is the IP right holder and that rights are being infringed or infringement is imminent. Such provisional measures may also include the right holder being required to provide a security or equivalent assurance partly to protect the defendant and/or to prevent abuse of enforcement rights.

Time-limits for proceedings

Provisional measures taken against the defendant to prevent the continued infringement may, upon the request of the defendant, be revoked or otherwise cease, unless proceedings leading to a decision on the merits of the case have not been initiated within reasonable time. The guideline for legal proceedings to commence should not exceed 20 working days or 31 calender days, whichever is the longer.

8.9 National border measures

In instances where intellectual property owners have valid grounds for suspecting importation of counterfeit trade mark or pirated copyright goods the right holder may lodge a written application with the appropriate authorities, for the customs authorities to suspend the release of such counterfeit goods into free circulation. The same option will be available for goods destined for exportation from the national customs territory.

The applicant of a customs suspension order will need to provide adequate evidence that under the laws of the country of importation, there is prima facie (at first sight) an obvious infringement of the intellectual property rights of the owner. The application must include a sufficiently detailed description of the infringing goods to make them easily recognisable to the customs authority.

In line with general provisional measures the applicant may be required to provide security or equivalent assurance to protect the defendant and prevent abuse of the suspension measures.

Where customs authorities suspend the release of goods involving industrial design, patents or undisclosed information into free circulation, a period not exceeding 10 working days before the goods will be released allow for legal proceedings to be initiated. In appropriate cases this time limit may be extended.

For cases of counterfeit trade mark goods, the authorities must not allow the reimportation of the infringing goods in an unaltered state or by subjecting the goods to a different customs procedure.

Rights of the importer and the owner of goods

Should the import detention order at a later date prove to be wrongful, the applicant may be ordered to pay the importer, the consignee and the owner of the goods appropriate compensation for any injury caused.

Alternatively, where the import prevention is rightly imposed the competent authorities shall provide the IP owner sufficient opportunity to have any goods detained by customs inspected in order to substantiate the owner's infringement claims.

Ex officio action

Individual TRIPs nations may decide to authorise their customs authorities to act upon their own initiative, giving the right to suspend the release of goods of which customs have received prima facie evidence from IP owners in respect of the infringement.

For such purposes the customs authorities may at any time seek information from the right holder to enable them to exercise their suspension powers. This is a particularly welcome provision by the TRIPs agreement, compared to earlier requirements, for right holders to give excessively detailed import information of the alleged infringement products such as the date and time of arrival of a consignment.

Where customs act upon their own initiative to suspend an importation (or exportation) of what they believe to be infringing goods, both the importer and IP right holder must be promptly informed. Giving the importer the option of lodging an appeal for the release of goods following the 10-day period for further legal proceedings to be initiated by the right holder.

International co-operation

Co-operation on an international scale is seen as being particularly important in the elimination of the international trade in goods infringing intellectual property rights. In particular, countries shall promote the exchange of information and co-operation between customs authorities in connection to counterfeit trade mark goods and pirated copyright goods.

8.10 Criminal procedures

Criminal procedures and penalties must be provided by TRIPs' individual member states, to be applied at least in cases where wilful or intentional trade mark counterfeiting or copyright piracy have taken place on a commercial scale.

Remedies available for criminal action must include imprisonment and/or monetary fines of a scale which will act as a substantial deterrent for possible counterfeit operations and individuals. Other action points will include the seizure, forfeiture and destruction of infringing goods and materials.

8.11 Legislation and transitional developments

The legislation, final judicial decisions and administrative procedures generally used for implementing the TRIPs agreement at national levels are required to be made available to governments and intellectual property holders throughout membership nations. The Council of TRIPs in Geneva must be notified of laws and regulations, while the WIPO is to establish a central register holding all such documents and information in connection with the TRIPs member countries.

With regard to the structure of a general dispute settlement, developments will continue to shape the final framework over a period of five years (until the year 2000). During this time the Council of TRIPs will be examining the scope and mechanics of such legal structure, before the submission of recommendations to the Ministerial Conference taking place every two years.

TRIPs Council and Ministerial Conference

After the high media profile of the Uruguay Round, establishment of the WTO plus signing of the TRIPs agreement in April 1994, the implementation and progress of the agreement may appear among the general public to have become somewhat subdued. However, a review of the latest TRIPs Council year report reveals that the ongoing implementation of this international agreement has far from slowed down. Throughout 1996 formal Council meetings took place every two months, to review and assess the progress of all TRIPs members in relation to the time schedule of the multilateral agreement. Examples of the Council's progress include:

- Co-operation agreement between TRIPs and the WIPO (enforced January 1, 1996) regarding the notification, access to and translation of national laws and regulations of TRIPs members thereby establishing a central information point for national legislations concerning intellectual property and related subjects.
- Review of 29 member countries national legislation, during a four-day Council meeting.
- Over half of all 123 TRIPs members had by the end of 1996 notified the Council of their official contact point(s) (regarding exchange of information and customs co-operation) for the purposes of co-operating with each other to eliminate international trade in goods infringing IP rights.

Points of recommendations made for the first Ministerial Conference (Singapore, December 9–13, 1996) included:

- Affirmation of the importance of full TRIPs implementation by each member within the agreed time-scales.
- Affirmation that to fully implement the Agreement the importance of developed countries to assist with technical assistance and co-operation to implement and update national legislations in developing and least-developed countries (according to independent arrangement between two member countries).

The official Singapore Ministerial Declaration included both the above affirmations and highlighted the purpose of integration of developing countries in the multilateral trading system 'is important for *their* [developing countries] economic development and for the global trade expansion [for all Member countries]'.

Transitional developments

Transitional arrangements within the TRIPs agreement also allow developing country member states a period of four years to make provisions within national legislation to meet the requirements and structure of the intellectual property agreement. Whereas for developed/industrialised countries the TRIPs agreement came into force from January 1995.

In the instance of least-developed country members a time-span of 10 years from the implementation of the TRIPs agreement (January, 1995) means that the minimum requirements of these countries involve granting the same rights 'no less favourable' to membership nationals as currently awarded to the country's own nationals. These transitional arrangements have been made in view of countries' economic, financial and administrative constraints whilst allowing time for their need for flexibility to create a viable technological base.

To facilitate the implementation of the TRIPs agreement developed nations shall, upon request and under mutually agreed terms, assist in the preparation of laws and regulations on the protection and enforcement of intellectual property rights as well as the prevention of their abuse. Support should also include the establishment or reinforcement of domestic offices and agencies, plus the training of personnel in the matters of intellectual property.

Through the international co-operation between highly and least-developed countries the advantage of 'tried and tested' legislative structures and procedures will hopefully encourage the strong protection of industrial intellectual property to spread throughout the nations—with significant benefits for companies producing and exporting industrial design products on an international level.

8.12 Conclusion

Although the TRIPs agreement came into force in January 1996, the extreme levels of diversity between different country members' legislations mean that the full implementation of the international IP agreement requires considerable time. Hence, the transitional time allowances of between one, four and 10 years for different levels of countries to adjust and establish a general legal framework which will satisfy the TRIPs structure.

For some countries this will require only small adjustments of current IP legislation, while other nations with no or very little legislation for intellectual property similar to the TRIPs structure must introduce considerable amounts of new legal measures and regulations within the transitional time scale of 10 years for least developed nations. However, in may be argued that with the TRIPs agreement already covering the major categories of intellectual property in a very detailed manner, it would be advantageous for all country members concerned that the TRIPs legal and enforcement framework is put in place sooner rather than later to even out current differences between member states and their individual legislations. The earliest possible adherence to the international agreement may also prevent owners of original design and trade mark products hesitating from sourcing and producing abroad, if intellectual property protection remains weak for a prolonged period of time.

To assess the effects of the TRIPs agreement, industry organisations Euratex (the European Apparel and Textile Organisation) and ATMI (the American Textile Manufacturers Institute) met in Geneva during 1996. With the purpose of exchanging views on the first 18 months of the Uruguay Round Textiles and Apparel Agreement plus views regarding the TRIPs agreement to be presented in connection to the WTO Ministerial Conference held in Singapore, December 1996. The initial viewpoint expressed from the Euratex and ATMI meeting indicated certain points of concern.

In relation to the subject of intellectual property protection and enforcement the ATMI Executive Vice President found that; 'Several developing countries are mainly interested in increasing their exports to the USA and the EU but pay little attention to their obligations in such areas as access to their own markets, subsidies, protection of intellectual property or control of Customs fraud . . . ' (*Textile Horizons*, June/July 1996).

On a larger scale governmental bodies are proceeding to ensure various countries meet and adhere to the obligations of the TRIPs agreement. In spring 1996, for example, the European Commission announced that it was to initiate proceedings in the World Trade Organisation against Japan for failing to meet the full 50-year copyright protection, in line with the TRIPs rules. The general implications should be seen as a critical test of the value of the WTO rules and of whether the individual nations will respect them.

Whilst taking note of the standpoint of industry organisations and test case action by the EU, on balance major newspapers have also reported that already *two months after* the Uruguay GATT agreement (including TRIPs) had been signed company managers noticed 'countries like Korea, India, Malaysia and China much more helpful . . . (than in the past)' with the whole area of intellectual property in consumer goods industries starting to shift rapidly.

In practical terms, while new international IP agreements continue to develop, the outline and details described for the UK and EU countries seem to give a clear indication that substantial protection of intellectual property *is* a realistic option for designers and businesses who want to protect their design and brand name assets effectively.

This is supported by the overall trend both in the UK and the European market, for legislation to become accessible and more 'user-friendly', to ensure designers and commercial management are able to apply and make use of the legislation as a business tool for protecting design investments.

As indicated in several parts of this book, various information points and organisations exist both in the UK and abroad that are able to assist in dealing with general questions, legal guidelines and disputes involving the protection of intellectual property. It is hoped that the book's Address List will go some way towards helping the reader to source further information/guidelines. Whereas legislation information for overseas countries may have to be obtained directly from national patent offices or the WTO central register for national legislation, an initial point of reference for many UK intellectual property owners will be the Patent Office (see contact details in Address List on pages 171–173).

The Patent Office, having adopted, in 1992, a customer service mission statement in order to achieve the distinction of being the *most effective* information service in the world, is certainly highly recommended both for individual designers and businesses. The central enquiry desk will be able to assist with most queries in *any* field of intellectual property, or alternatively be able to advise which organisation to contact for further legal advice.

ADDRESS LIST

United Kingdom organisations concerned with intellectual property protection

Anti Copying in Design (A©ID)
c/o Theodore Goddard, 150 Aldersgate Street, London EC1A 4EJ
Tel: +(0)171 606 8855 Fax: +(0)171 606 4390
e-mail: tg@link.org

British Copyright Council
Copyright House, 29–33 Berners Street, London W1P 4AA

British Science Reference Library & Information Services
25 Southampton Buildings, London WC2A 1AW
Tel: +(0)171 323 7494

Chartered Institute of Patent Agents
Staple Inn Buildings, High Holborn, London WC1V 7PZ
Tel: +(0)171 405 9450 Fax: +(0)171 430 0471
e-mail: mailatcipa.org.uk

Chartered Society of Designers (CSD)
32–38 Saffron Hill, London EC1N 8FH
Tel: +(0)171 831 9777 Fax: +(0)171 831 6277

Clothing Namecheck
Linder Myers Solicitors (Attn: Trevor Bell)
Phoenix House, 45 Cross Street, Manchester M2 4JF
Tel: +(0)161 832 6972 Fax: +(0)161 834 0718
e-mail: linder_myers@uk.pipeline.com

Commission of the European Communities
Jean Monnet House, 8 Storey's House, London SW1 3AT
Tel: +(0)171 973 1992 Fax: +(0)171 973 1900

Design and Artists Copyright Society (DACS)
Parchment House, 13 Northburgh Street, London EC1V 0AH
Tel: +(0)171 336 8811 Fax: +(0)171 336 8822

Fashion Design Protection Associates (FDPA)
25 Watsons Road, Wood Green, London N22 4TE
Tel: +(0)181 888 1213 Fax: +(0)181 889 8736

Institute of Trade Marks Agents (ITMA)
Canterbury House, 2–6 Sydenham Road, Croydon, Surrey CR0 9XE
Tel: +(0)181 686 2052 Fax: +(0)181 680 5723

Patent Office (including The Design Registry & Trade Mark Registry)
The Patent Office, 25 Southampton Buildings, Chancery Lane, London WC2A 1AY and the Patent Office, Cardiff Road, Newport, Gwent NP9 1RH

Main enquiry desk   Tel: +(0)645 500 505 (local call rate)
Copyright enquiries Tel: +(0)171 438 4777
Design enquiry desk Tel: +(0)1633 811 161
Patent enquiry desk Tel: +(0)171 438 4700 (London)
                     +(0)1633 813 932 (Newport)
Trade mark enquiries Tel: +(0)01633 814 706/9

International/overseas organisations concerned with intellectual property protection

European Patent Information and Documentation Systems (EPIDOS)
Schottenfeldgasse 29, Postfach 82, A–1072 Vienna, Austria
Tel: +43 1 521 26-40 51 or -406 Fax: +43 1 52126-41 92
e-mail: infowien@epo.e-mail.com

Other EPIDOS Information Services:
Germany/Munich   Tel: +49 89 23 99 45 12
Germany/Berlin   Tel: +49 30 25 901-111
Netherlands/The Hague   Tel: +31 70 340 32 54

European Patent Office (EPO)
Erhardtstrasse 27, D–80331 Munich, Germany.
Tel: +49 89 23 99 0 Fax: +49 8923 99 44 65
World Wide Web—EPO information pages: http://www.epo.co.at/epo/

Office for Harmonisation in the Internal Market (OHIM)
(European Trade Marks and Designs)
Avenida de Aguilera 20, E–03080 Alicante, Spain
Telephone helpline: +34 6 513 9333 Fax: +34 6 513 1344

US Copyright Office
Copyright Office, Publications Section, LM–455, Library of Congress, Washington DC, 20559, USA
Tel: +1 202 707 3000. Forms and publications hotline: +1 202 707 9100

Alternatively US Copyright application forms and assistance from:
Law Offices of L H Stein, United States and International Attorneys of Law, 5th Floor, 10 Eastcheap, London EC3M 1ET
Tel: +(0)171 623 3229 Fax: +(0)171 623 3227
e-mail: 71260.2222@compuserve.com

World Intellectual Property Organisation (WIPO)
34 Chemin des Colombetttes, PO Box 18, CH–1211 Geneva 20, Switzerland
Tel: +41 22 730 9111 Fax: +41 22 740 1435
Fax (International Trade Mark Registry): +41 22 740 1429

World Trade Organisation (WTO)
Intellectual Property and Investment Division, Centre William Rappard, Rue de Lausanne 154, CH–1211 Geneva 21, Switzerland
Tel: +41 22 739 51 11 Fax: +41 22 739 57 90
World Wide Web—WTO information pages: http://www.unicc.org/wto/

REFERENCES

1. D'Archirafi, V. (EEC Commissioner—Internal Market) (1991) 'Green Paper on the Legal Protection of Industrial Design', French and English publication by Comitextil, *EC Bulletin* **6**, 34–74.
2. Design and Artists Copyright Society (DACS) (1993) *Copyright Protection and Remedies for Infringement including Textiles, Fabrics and Clothing*, Fact Sheet.
3. Fashion Design Protection Associates Ltd (FDPA) (1996) FDPA Memorandum—on the Law of Copyright and Design Right, © FDPA London.
4. Fashion Design Protection Associates Ltd (FDPA) (1996) Some information on the Fashion Protection Associates Limited, © FDPA London.
5. Patent Office, The: Design Registration, DTI, Publication: 836, 1991 London.
6. Patent Office, The: Basic Facts—Copyright, DTI, Publication: 878, 1992 London.
7. Patent Office, The:Basic Facts—Designs, DTI, Publication: 876, 1992 London.
8. Patent Office, The: Basic Facts—Patents, DTI, Publication 877, 1992 London.
9. Patent Office, The: Basic Facts—Registered Trade and Service Marks, DTI, Publication: 875, 1992 London.
10. Patent Office, The: Registering A Trade or Service Mark, DTI, Publication 1404, 1994 London.
11. Patent Office, The: What is intellectual property, DTI, Publication: 874/20K/1/92. 1992 London.

12. Patent Office, The: Patent Protection, DTI Publication 1244, 1993
     London.
13. Pipe, Paulette: The Protection Factor, pp 38–39, Drapers Record,
     11/04/1992, EMAP Fashion. London.

BIBLIOGRAPHY

UK intellectual property legislation

Copyright, Designs and Patents Act 1988 (238 pages), HMSO publication, London. ISBN 0-10-544888-5.
Trade Marks Act 1994 (66 pages), HMSO publication, London. ISBN 0-10-542694-6.

European Community design regulation

Proposal for a European Parliament and Council Regulation on Community Design (30 pages), 94C 29/02, Official Journal of the European Communities, January 31, 1994.
Common Position (EC) 1997, On the Legal Protection of Designs (18 pages), 6401/97, Directive adopted by the Internal Market Council, March 13, 1997.

WTO—TRIPs agreement

Agreement on Trade-Related Aspects of Intellectual Property Rights (29 pages),
Treaty Series, HMSO publication, London. ISBN 0-10-130462-5.

INDEX